"*Global Revival* is an engrossing account of the 1902 Melbourne evangelistic mission and how it fueled revival fires locally and throughout the world. This book combines careful historical analysis with extremely readable prose. The result is a book that pulsates (even in its details) with recollections of a historical moment when God's Spirit moved in powerful ways to draw people to Christ and rekindle his church. Those of us who long and pray for revival will discover in this book a helpful account of how God worked in the past along with principles for how he might do so again in the future."

—KENNETH BERDING,
professor of New Testament, Talbot School of Theology, Biola University

"Robert J. Nyhuis in *Global Revival* has produced a superb historical study that speaks to us clearly and directly of the great spiritual need of today's secular societies. The author introduces readers to a little-known antipodean gem of God's glory that launched a global awakening in this delightfully readable and lively analysis of the 1902 R. A. Torrey revival meetings in Melbourne, Victoria. Filled with vivid prose and accompanied by original photographs, sermons, and letters along with study questions, this book has conveyed a living sense of Torrey the Chicagoan evangelist and the Melbourne revival within a socio-cultural context that many will realize they only thought they knew."

—ROBERT L. GALLAGHER,
professor emeritus of intercultural studies, A. Duane Litfin Divinity School, Wheaton College Graduate School, Chicago

"Robert J. Nyhuis provides a compelling exploration of the 1902 Melbourne Revival, unpacking its dynamics, the scope of its impact, and the lessons we can apply today. It is an inspiring and insightful read."

—MARK SAYERS,
author of *Reappearing Church*

"This is the story of one of the most significant revivals known to history. In it was sown the seeds of the more famous Welsh Revival of 1904/5 and of other revivals in four continents in the first decade of the twentieth century. This revival was in a fifth continent: Australia. Not only does it deserve to be better known, but the fullest contemporary records of it exist, and this well-researched account is based on their solid foundation. Here we are told, with clarity and comprehensiveness, its background, how it was organized and supported in prayer, who led it and spoke at it, the character and gifts of its preachers, what they said (an appendix contains five of the addresses delivered during the revival), how its message was received, the impact it made on Australian society and the church, and how it ignited revival fires in other nations throughout the world. By focusing on this one revival, Robert Nyhuis has done a great service for all who long for revival, all who wonder how Jesus, 'the desire of the nations,' could satisfy the heart hunger of the Australian nation today, and how the Australian church could again be a blessing to the other continents of the earth. Are the knowledge of past revivals and the expectation that the Lord will do it again in the future rising in Australia? This authoritative analysis is well calculated to raise that exciting prospect even higher."

—STUART PIGGIN,
associate professor, Centre for the History of Christian Thought and Experience, Macquarie University

Global Revival

Global Revival

How a City's Mission Catalyzed a Worldwide Awakening

ROBERT J. NYHUIS

RESOURCE *Publications* · Eugene, Oregon

GLOBAL REVIVAL
How a City's Mission Catalyzed a Global Awakening

Copyright © 2025 Robert J. Nyhuis. All rights reserved. Except for brief quotations in critical publications or reviews, no part of this book may be reproduced in any manner without prior written permission from the publisher. Write: Permissions, Wipf and Stock Publishers, 199 W. 8th Ave., Suite 3, Eugene, OR 97401.

Resource Publications
An Imprint of Wipf and Stock Publishers
199 W. 8th Ave., Suite 3
Eugene, OR 97401

www.wipfandstock.com

PAPERBACK ISBN: 979-8-3852-4039-5
HARDCOVER ISBN: 979-8-3852-4040-1
EBOOK ISBN: 979-8-3852-4041-8
VERSION NUMBER 02/19/25

All Scripture quotations, unless otherwise indicated, are taken from the Authorized Version of the Holy Bible.

This book is dedicated to my wife, Anna, whose unfailing patience and constant encouragement has supported me throughout the production of this work.

Contents

List of Illustrations | viii

Preface | ix

Acknowledgments | xi

1. Characteristics of Revival | 1
2. Background to Revival | 12
3. Preparations for Revival | 29
4. Four Weeks of Revival Impact | 44
5. Leadership of Revival | 66
6. The Transforming Revival Message | 83
7. From Local to Global Revival | 98
8. Revival Revisited | 116

Appendix 1: Timeline of Events | 123

Appendix 2: Selected Sermons | 125

Appendix 3: Spots | 152

Appendix 4: Letter to Hannah MacNeil | 154

Appendix 5: Mission Districts (Published in The Age 12th April 1902, 14.) | 157

Appendix 6: Summary of Suburban Mission Reports | 160

Appendix 7: Program for Torrey and Alexander Valedictory Meetings | 167

Bibliography | 169

List of Illustrations

Alexander's Choir at an Exhibition Building service | 58

Alexander's Choir beneath the advertisement of the Y.M.C.A. service with W. E. Geil | 58

R. A. Torrey | 59

W. E. Geil | 59

Charles M. Alexander | 59

S. Pearce Carey (Mission Chairperson) | 59

Exhibition Building, 1902 | 60

Exhibition Building, 2024 | 60

Melbourne Town Hall, 1902 | 61

Melbourne Town Hall, 2024 | 61

The 'Glory Song' (from the first edition of *Alexander's Revival Songs*, 1902) | 62

Interior of a Suburban meeting held at the Federal Hall, Footscray | 63

Interior of the Exhibition Building | 63

Robert Harkness, mission pianist and Torrey biographer | 64

Evangelization Society of Victoria with James Balfour, President (upper right), Charles Carter, Secretary (bottom right), and G. P. Barber (front row, second from left) | 64

Southern Cross (1902 masthead) | 65

Southern Cross (special edition) | 65

West Melbourne tent mission with Robert Robertson | 65

Preface

In 1902, a local revival in Melbourne, in the Australian state of Victoria, saw 8,642 conversions in just four weeks. Decision cards helped to consolidate professions of faith along with discussion and prayer after daily revival services. Most of the conversions were secured in the very building that had, less than a year prior, been the venue for the official opening of Parliament after the nation's federation. Churches concerned at increasing secularism and widespread despair after a recent economic downturn had been expressing hunger for a religious revival to transform the city.

Prayer was a significant foundation for the event which was preceded by gatherings of 16,800 groups over seven weeks (more than two thousand weekly), which interceded for the salvation of the city. A gathering of local ministers had prayed at length each week since 1889, even after the death of their leader in 1896. The 1902 Mission's keynote speaker, R. A. Torrey, had replaced famed evangelist, D. L. Moody, as head of his Bible Institute and Chicago church. More recently, Torrey had also held prayer meetings for worldwide revival for three years.

Melbourne's 'Simultaneous Mission' had planned for two weeks of evangelism in some fifty suburban venues, with the aim of personally inviting every household to the services being conducted. Meetings would mostly be held in tents and public halls to make attendance easier for those not accustomed to regular involvement in churches. The climax of the Mission would then be two weeks of evening services in the city's center where attendances would exceed 8,000 nightly, with hundreds being turned away. Lunchtime gatherings, initially for businessmen, and later also for women, would swell in excess of 5,000 people meeting in their lunch hour. No less than 214 churches from most denominations keenly participated in the greatest show of ecumenism Melbourne had known in its short history.

Preface

Torrey, joined by little-known sprightly Pennsylvanian evangelist, W. E. Geil, and the magnetic and talented choir master from Tennessee, Charles Alexander, caused a stir that reverberated well beyond the month-long Mission schedule. That other events of this nature had been known through Moody's earlier influence in the U.S.A. and the United Kingdom (with recent examples in England, but also in Sydney) might have rendered Melbourne's Mission little more than an earnest replica event. It was, however, the scale of its impact and the continuity of its preparatory prayer that perpetuated a wave of revival across parts of Australia and New Zealand, then quickly stirring a widespread awakening that touched India, England, Wales, Scotland, Ireland, Europe, South America, and the U.S.A.

This is the story of how one city's Simultaneous Mission, today unknown to most of its inhabitants, was able with the leadership of three international evangelists to catalyze a worldwide revival phenomenon. It is a story minimally heeded, but a story whose lessons must surely be recaptured by an increasingly secular generation. More than a century on, the impact of those four stunning weeks reveals key principles by which cities might once again be stirred to passionately respond to the proclamation of the Christian Gospel.

Rob Nyhuis
December 2024

Acknowledgments

My colleagues and friends at the Churches of Christ demonstrate a passion for mission which emulates that seen in the personalities of 1902 described in this book. Their support and encouragement to me is greatly appreciated.

I wish to thank those who have assisted with the provision of material used in writing this work, including the staff and volunteers of the State Library of Victoria, the Archives Collection of the Uniting Church Records and Historical Society of Victoria, the Archives Collection of the Billy Graham Center, and the Doylestown Historical Society.

Thanks, too, to Barry Chant, Stuart Piggin, Ken Berding, Mark Sayers, and Robert Gallagher for their inspiration and kind words.

1.
Characteristics of Revival

On the Threshold of Revival?

Reuben Archer Torrey stood at 9:45 pm on Friday 11th April in 1902 preparing to speak to a large gathering of 2,500 people assembled in Melbourne's Town Hall.[1] The waiting crowd, unfazed by the lateness of his address, stood to its feet and welcomed their distinguished American guest with cheering. Torrey recognized that something significant was about to unfold in the weeks ahead. The air of anticipation filled not only the building, but the entire city. Representatives from 214 participating churches and 700 local committees joined the event's presently-assembled volunteer workers and choir members. Some 117,000 people had also been in attendance at 16,800 home prayer meetings – more than two thousand per

---

1. Williamson, *A Great Revival*, 24; *Southern Cross*, 18th April 1902, 435. The journey of the 1902 Simultaneous Mission was charted by the *Southern Cross*, a weekly newspaper produced in Melbourne from 1874 to 1928 and edited for most of its life by W. H. Fitchett, a prominent Methodist. It was an inter-denominational publication presenting an evangelical perspective on local and global issues. Torrey later described it as "the best religious paper" he had ever seen and Geil further advocated its promotional use, advising, "get a stack of the *Southern Cross* and send them to your friends" (5th June 1902, 21). The paper's measured commentary sees it compare favorably with accounts of the Mission from other sources, including the brief sympathetic coverage found in major daily newspapers. Although Melbourne's satirical *Punch* found occasion for criticism of aspects of the mission, even this newspaper complimented Torrey's opening address as "a perfect sermon" (17th April 1902). A full set of copies of the *Southern Cross* survives only on microfilm at the State Library of Victoria in Melbourne, Australia. Its detailed coverage of key events in the decades prior to the 1902 Mission remains invaluable in authenticating much of the religious climate of the period. (Page numbers out of sequence refer to special editions published on 5th June and 10th September 1902).

week over a seven-week period – in preparing for the success of an unparalleled four-week mission. It was to feature keynote American evangelists, Torrey, William Edgar Geil, and singer, Charles M. Alexander, along with multiple other preachers.[2] A staggering 8,642 converts would be recorded in Melbourne's four weeks of services.[3] This 'Simultaneous Mission' was so-named because it was about to touch some fifty urban centers for two weeks. It would then culminate in another fortnight of services in both the Town Hall and the city's flagship venue, the majestic Exhibition Building. Less than twelve months prior it had hosted the opening of the nation's inaugural Parliament following the federation of the Australian colonies.

With the present event unadvertised, for fear that the public would swamp the venue before the coming weekend launch, Torrey now spoke to an expectant crowd. Those attending had already pledged to "speak the name of Jesus reverently to at least one person during the next twenty-four hours."[4] Affirming the organizers and the previous weeks of concerted prayer, Torrey also acknowledged the intercessions of 5,000 others outside Australia who were praying for the event's success.[5] Perhaps no mission of such size and scope had ever before adopted such intense cooperation and unity. Torrey was confident of significant impact.

> *I am waiting for the day that shall [arrive] when word shall come from all fifty Mission centers, saying that as this man or that man of God was speaking, God honored His Word, and the Holy Spirit did His work. We shall not be satisfied with a few thousand conversions in this city. What we are looking for, and what I am confident we are going to see, is the Spirit of God coming to every township, village and city in every State . . .*[6]

During the evening, the fifty divisional leaders from each local mission center had risen to further applause. Six spoke to the crowd along with several of the key organizers. Event chairman, S. Pearce Carey, spoke despite suffering an illness. An appeal was made for the balance of the financial cost of

---

2. *Southern Cross*, 18th April 1902, 423; *Argus*, 12th April 1902, 19; *Spectator* 18th April 1902, 555.

3. Torrey, *The Power of Prayer*, 49. The number was approximated at 8,500 in the *Southern Cross* souvenir edition (10th September 1902, 28) and at 8,600 by biographer, George T. B. Davis (*Torrey and Alexander*, 81).

4. *Southern Cross*, 18th April 1902, 434.

5. *Southern Cross*, 10th September 1902, 8–9.

6. *Southern Cross*, 18th April 1902, 434. Note that the various Australian states were recognized as colonies before the nation's federation in 1901.

Characteristics of Revival

the Mission to avoid receiving offerings in the presence of those who would attend evening services, after donations had also been received in the home prayer meetings and at the Mission's central office.[7] A pledge slip had been made available, being included in the *Southern Cross*, Melbourne's weekly evangelical newspaper, for ease of contribution. It declared the estimated cost to be £2,500 for the fifty preliminary missions and sought completion of a pledge: "Sympathising with the objects of the above movement, and appreciating the desire to have all necessary funds in hand before the Mission commences, I have pleasure in forwarding herewith the sum of . . ." A space was made available for the amount, date, signature, and address of donors, with a footnoted request that contributions be forwarded to the secretaries at the Mission office situated in the city's pre-eminent Baptist church facility.[8]

Carey believed that the Mission might well be undermined by public requests for large sums of money, as had happened in previous events. He proceeded instead to ask all workers gathered at the Mission's launch for an advance contribution that would eradicate the overall debt. Widespread support was evidenced by more than £3,000 eventually being raised, with one-third being received in threepenny bits.[9] The *Southern Cross* documented Carey's appeal.

> "I am going to ask you to pay £500 now," said Mr. Carey, and there was a stir right through the Hall. "Does that scare you?" asked the chairman. "Hands up those who will give 5s. 6d. – that's the average amount required from this audience to clear the whole expenses." Some 200 or 300 hands went up. "Those who cannot afford 5s. 6d. but will promise special help, hands up!" Several hundred more hands were raised, and an assurance given that at least a considerable proportion of the necessary funds would be forthcoming.[10]

At the same event, Carey also commended the collaboration of Christians across the city who had previously pledged unity at similar events, ones nevertheless attended by fewer people.

> "We have allowed our denominational differences to stand aside and have combined to preach the Cross of Christ, and we have found intense delight in such cooperation . . . The last time we met there

---

7. *Southern Cross*, 21st March 1902, 327.
8. *Southern Cross*, 11th April 1902, 402.
9. *Punch*, 22nd May 1902, 9.
10. *Southern Cross*, 18th April 1902, 434.

> were 300 present, and the change from 300 to 2,000 represents the increase and spread of interest in the Mission and shows, too, how the workers are multiplying, and how the churches are being stirred to their depths."[11]

Successor to the celebrated trans-Atlantic evangelist, Dwight Lyman Moody, Torrey hailed from Chicago where he was busily engaged with the leadership of Moody's former church and his growing Bible Institute when approached to come to Australia. What became a four-year international revival journey, leading to tens of thousands of converts to faith, was kindled in prayer and ignited in Melbourne. What was soon referred to as the "Great Revival"[12] became the key initial component of a national, and then international, awakening that had arisen despite economic hardship and evidence of increased secularism.

Simultaneous Missions had already involved Christians across many world cities banding together for concentrated evangelistic forays, riding a wave of some "fifty years of evangelical advance."[13] The Keswick holiness preacher and contemporary of Moody, F. B. Meyer, summed up the gravity of these events as understood by their participants.

> During the mission the missioner should feel set apart for a very solemn purpose. He should disengage himself as far as possible from the pressure of correspondence and literary work, that he may give himself to prayer and the ministry of the Word. There must be a certain restraint from the ordinary commonplaces of life, that the whole soul may be gathered up, with girt loins, for its sacred duties. Of course, there should be exercise, the vigorous walk into the country, the light enjoyment of the amenities and humanities that come naturally in the routine of daily living, the frolic with the children of the home. But anything like mere sight-seeing, excursion-making, relaxed intercourse with men or women, excess in eating or drinking, will sensibly diminish the spiritual power and unfit the soul.[14]

Historians, Stuart Piggin and Robert Linder, see the mission in Melbourne as having been an early "part of a wider revival movement, one of many tributaries which flowed into what amounted to the greatest of evangelical

---

11. *Southern Cross*, 18th April 1902, 433.
12. Warren, "Genesis," 201.
13. Orr, *Evangelical Awakenings*, 97.
14. *Southern Cross*, 21st March 1902, 318.

awakenings, that of the first decade of the twentieth century."[15] A 1901 nationwide mission in England had been followed by the Simultaneous Mission of Sydney in November of that year. Each was characterized by stories of significant impact. Notably, a famous and subsequent Welsh Revival story of the colliery pit ponies that had failed to recognize the commands of converted miners who had stopped swearing was also being reported at the continuing revival south of Sydney in early 1902.[16] Melbourne's own mission was to build on the accumulated learnings of these prior events but, importantly, would utilise prolonged preparatory prayer and the skills and experience of prominent international evangelists in garnering results unlike those ever seen in earlier Missions.

Awakening or Revival?

'Awakening' as a specific term describing historical religious revitalization is perhaps only minimally used today in describing optimized mission in contemporary contexts. Alternative descriptors, such as 'revival,' are often preferred.[17] Are the two terms interchangeable? For Colin Whittaker, revivals are identified as "those special seasons of divine visitation when God the Holy Ghost quickens and stirs the slumbering Church of God."[18] By definition, a 'revival' contemplates a restoration of life, with 'awakenings' often referring instead to widespread community impact resulting from revivals.[19] Mark Stibbe sees religious awakening transcending personal salvation and specifically involving community transformation.[20] Darrell Paproth helpfully reconciles these terms by characterising awakenings as revivals on a larger scale.[21] Melbourne's Simultaneous Mission may be understood, then,

---

15. Piggin and Linder, *The Fountain of Public Prosperity*, 530.

16. *Illawarra Mercury*, 26th February 1902, 2. Stead later reported that the pit ponies of miners converted during the Welsh Revival were intentionally "retrained to do their work without the incentive of profanity" (*The Welsh Revival*, 42).

17. Nigel Scotland finds a gap between the biblical references to revival as spiritual renewal or refreshing and the contemporary framing of revival as "a powerful intensification of God's saving work in and through his people," occurring periodically with evidence of conversion and holiness ("Towards a Biblical Understanding," 122).

18. Whittaker, *Great Revivals*, 21.

19. Whittaker, *Great Revivals*, 21 cf. 23–33.

20. Stibbe, "No Limits, No Boundaries," 235.

21. Paproth, "Revivalism in Melbourne," 145.

as a local revival of Christian spiritual vitality, albeit at a time when 96% of the population at least nominally identified as Christian.[22]

Piggin and Linder nevertheless use the term 'revival' more generically when describing any event characterized by a "unique" and "unexpected" peak experience of God who serves as the source of its power in proclaiming the Gospel.[23] Piggin has also observed revival as a work of the Spirit among large numbers of people in "convicting, converting and regenerating."[24] In the absence of universal precision, though, the two terms, 'revival' and 'awakening,' are used synonymously herein. They describe the general renewal of enthusiasm for Christian spirituality which, while promoting personal devotion, is associated with widespread community evangelism and impact within a defined period.

Such transformative events described as revivals are often accompanied by penitence, humility, and persistent prayer, even though they are fundamentally also divine visitations.[25] Martyn Lloyd-Jones argues that, if the Spirit is deemed to have come in fullness at a believer's regeneration, then there would remain no room for the observable and repeated falling of the Spirit upon the Church, regardless of the necessity of the Spirit's work in those new to faith.[26] Human action in cooperating with the intent of the Spirit to empower afresh is therefore an exercise of free will that does not itself disregard the fact of God's sovereignty in bringing such revival. For Lloyd-Jones, this revival is a *continual* "revivifying" work of the Spirit in every Christian through intentional pursuit of an infilling, or baptism, with the Holy Spirit.[27] Despite the role of the Spirit in first bringing people to faith, then, the Spirit's work on each occasion of encounter remains one that is beyond human effort. That the importance of this work was so prominent in the ministry of Reuben Torrey cannot be divorced from his message or from the fruit of the Simultaneous Mission that increasingly came to be regarded as a revival.[28]

---

22. Coghlan, *Statistical Account 1901–1902*, 839.

23. Piggin and Linder, *The Fountain of Public Prosperity*, 332.

24. Piggin, "Towards a Theoretical Understanding," 17.

25. Lloyd-Jones, *Joy Unspeakable*, 276.

26. Lloyd-Jones, *Joy Unspeakable*, 279.

27. Lloyd-Jones, *Joy Unspeakable*, 280.

28. Lloyd-Jones makes this same observation in relation to the ministry of Moody (*Joy Unspeakable*, 210).

Leonard Ravenhill has nevertheless observed that revivals may be hindered because of quantifiable factors such as the commercialization of evangelism, carelessness in follow-up, fear of proclaiming truth, a lack of urgency in prayer, and a tendency for preachers to assume the glory for any successes which may eventuate.[29] Rather than suggesting that revivals might be manufactured with attendance to these factors, though, he indicates that human will is engaged with the intent that divine visitation be experienced. Geoffrey Treloar observes the significance of such intentionality in undergirding the divine impact experienced at the time.

> *Corporate evangelicalism reflected the emerging industrial capitalism of the era, in that, as in business, contract law, and engineering, it was about ascertaining what actually works in life and applying the resultant formulae to produce predictable and definite outcomes.*[30]

The 1902 event in Melbourne, which sought to apply lessons from previous revivals did nevertheless avoid the pitfalls identified by Ravenhill. Fundraising was almost entirely completed prior to its commencement, with the major people involved at pains to avoid profiteering. Coordinated planning by churches and the specific follow-up of converts helped to place them in local congregations as quickly as possible, but also therefore to recruit more assistance in this regard. Direct, and sometimes confrontational, preachers focused explicitly on a need to address sin and repentance and to preach for personal transformation. Prayer undergirded the mission with increased urgency for more than a decade prior to the event. Finally, the efforts of the key evangelists, detailed in the *Southern Cross*, revealed a self-effacing character and humility that was aligned to ecumenical unity and cooperation.

Characterizing and Cultivating Local Revivals

Almost six decades after the 1902 Simultaneous Mission the evangelist, Billy Graham, spoke prior to boarding an aircraft at the conclusion of his three month tour of Australia and New Zealand in 1959, known as the 'Southern Cross Crusade,'[31] declaring, "God has done great things in these

---

29. Ravenhill, *Why Revival Tarries*, 56–60.
30. Treloar, "The First Global Revivalist?" 883.
31. A reference to the common name of the prominent constellation, *Crux*, observable in the southern skies and depicted on the national flags of Australia and New Zealand.

lands beneath the southern stars, and to Him be the glory, praise and honor."[32] The visit resulted from "an overwhelming burden" by which he had felt led by the Holy Spirit to come[33] and included all the major cities of the two nations. Melbourne was the first city visited, with several locations used in the lead up to a final event at which an estimated crowd of 143,750 gathered on 15th March, the largest single crowd Graham had addressed to that point in time. He declared it to be "one of the greatest in the history of evangelism in the world."[34]

Piggin and Linder identify six characteristics of revival they believe were evident in 1959: the expectation of revival; unprecedented unity; extraordinary prayerfulness; a revitalized church; large numbers of converts; and the reduction of sinful practices in the community.[35] Quantified in the Australian context to show the impact of Graham's visit, these elements are difficult to project or measure more widely. Could they, and do they, exist within other revivals or missions? Firstly, a focus on the number of converts is perhaps easily measured for comparison, but genuine conversion becomes less concerned with initial responsiveness to an event and more with a considered commitment beyond it. The 1959 Melbourne visit by Graham, without having the benefit of momentum from the prior filling of venues in other cities, saw 28,105 personal responses to sessions across a four-week period when the city's population was almost 1.8 million.[36] It will be shown that a comparable statistic emerged from the 1902 Mission. Could this reflect the existence of common revival principles?

Secondly, regarding outcomes of the Graham visit, assessing any change in "sinful practices" might seem somewhat subjective, although Piggin and Linder specifically identify a reduction in alcohol consumption, exnuptial births, and convictions for crimes in Australia in the year following Graham's visit.[37] Such quantification may broadly be grouped with church revitalization to create a cluster of short-term social impact measures.

---

32. Babbage and Siggins, *Light Beneath the Cross*, 182.

33. Graham, *Just as I Am*, 325.

34. Babbage and Siggins, *Light Beneath the Southern Cross*, 23–4. Melbourne was the first city visited by Graham in Australasia, thus providing impetus for the remainder of the tour. Babbage and Siggins show that Melbourne's final event crowd total was estimated by the Melbourne Cricket Club, custodians of the venue used, the Melbourne Cricket Ground, which had hosted the 1956 Olympic Games.

35. Piggin and Linder, *Attending to the National Soul*, 278–89.

36. Babbage and Siggins, *Light Beneath the Southern Cross*, 27.

37. Piggin and Lindner, *Attending to the National Soul*, 287–8.

CHARACTERISTICS OF REVIVAL

Indeed, church memberships were widely reported to have increased, as did enrolments in Bible Colleges, such as in the Melbourne Bible Institute which claimed more than half its 1969 students to be products of the mission a decade prior.[38] Though Graham was reluctant to regard as revival a response rate of more than double the number of converts seen globally in prior years, he observed the associated spiritual hunger to be the greatest he had witnessed in his ministry to date.[39]

Furthermore, important factors of unity and prayerfulness may be paired, too, in considering the revival's ecumenical engagement in intentional preparation. Unprecedented unity was well-demonstrated during the Southern Cross Crusade as 'Operation Andrew' enacted a co-ordinated program of visitation and invitation, supported by many hundreds of churches and clergy.[40] The prayerfulness of the city was demonstrated by the organization of five hundred household prayer meetings, with more people allegedly praying internationally for the mission's success than had ever prayed for one place in history.[41] Graham himself advocated prayer as a key to spiritual awakening in Australia.[42]

Finally, the remaining dimension given by Piggin and Linder, the expectation of revival, was partially cultivated by the presence of an internationally well-known missioner and his transforming evangelistic message being widely promoted and anticipated. That this grouping of Piggin and Linder's six features of revival creates four key revival dimensions – large numbers of converts, notable community outcomes, ecumenical preparation, and the expectation associated with a transformative message by mission leaders – is suggestive of broader application. Could these dimensions be evidenced in accounts of the 1902 Mission, and are they replicable today? Also, could other factors potentially be at play?

Two Australian Christian historians, Darrell Paproth and Barry Chant, offer further insights on the characteristics of revival which may be relevant to the specific context of Melbourne in 1902. Noting similar features to those above derived from Piggin and Linder, Paproth argues for an understanding of revival at this time in terms of the characteristics of American Protestantism, with evidence of: spiritual vitality; the conversion

---

38. Piggin and Lindner, *Attending to the National Soul*, 284.
39. Piggin and Lindner, *Attending to the National Soul*, 285–6.
40. Babbage and Siggins, *Light Beneath the Southern Cross*, 17.
41. Babbage and Siggins, *Light Beneath the Southern Cross*, 17–18.
42. Babbage and Siggins, *Light Beneath the Southern Cross*, 18.

of unbelievers; organized mission; and large-scale impact at a specific point in time.[43] Torrey's measured style, however, made him better suited to receptivity by an audience attuned to conservative British influences.[44] Torrey offered austere intellectualism as opposed to the "excessive emotion" or "sensational evangelistic techniques" he observed in fellow American preachers of the era, such as Billy Sunday.[45]

In writing about the early development of Australian Pentecostalism, Chant cites the influence of Wesleyanism and visits by late nineteenth century evangelists in shaping evangelical receptivity.[46] Importantly, he observes revival as a localised phenomenon within Australia[47] and identifies characteristics of revival somewhat similar to those of Paproth: spiritual revitalization as a sovereign act of God; an experience of New Testament Christianity inclusive of significant evangelistic impact; an outcome resulting from preparation that is both careful and spiritual; and the historical convergence of events and circumstances.[48] While overlapping with the findings of Paproth and of Piggin and Linder, Chant does prefer to describe his localized awakenings as divine time-bound visitations, understanding revival itself to be an idealized ongoing expression of New Testament faith, as for Lloyd-Jones.[49]

The traits quantified by Piggin and Linder in relation to the Graham visit are largely reconcilable with those offered by both Paproth and Chant in offering four important features of revival to be identified within the context of the same city, albeit that the two events under consideration existed decades apart. The following chapters will specifically follow these revival characteristics in the earlier four-week Melbourne Mission. Firstly, a distinctive and transformative message was evident in the ministries of the key personnel, utilizing purposeful organization and intentional delivery to create an expectation of revival. Secondly, there existed a commitment to ecumenical unity and prayerfulness by which spiritual vitality was generated. Thirdly, significant evangelistic fruitfulness was measurable, despite the variety of missioners and their backgrounds across the entire 1902

---

43. Paproth, "Revivalism in Melbourne," 144–5.
44. Paproth, "Revivalism in Melbourne," 162.
45. Marsden, *Fundamentalism and American Culture*, 130.
46. Chant, *The Spirit of Pentecost*, 83.
47. Chant, *The Spirit of Pentecost*, 26.
48. Chant, *This is Revival*, 28.
49. Chant, *This is Revival*, 74.

campaign. Fourthly, community transformation and local church revitalization was observable. Significantly, in the 1902 event, this involved the catalysis of global impact that largely replicated these four factors abroad.

United and energizing preparation and prayer, a transformative intentional message by prominent missioners, significant evangelistic fruitfulness, and broader social impact. These hallmarks of revival were uniquely outworked in a particular season of opportunity in Melbourne in 1902. After an initial examination of the background to this Simultaneous Mission, the relevance of these factors to contemporary revivalistic activity will then be examined in subsequent chapters.

Study Questions

1. How might churches cooperate again today in seeking to win people to faith? Can barriers of belief, geography, or logistics be overcome in fostering such unity?

2. To what extent does finance both help and hinder the spread of the Gospel? How might the example of Melbourne's approach to fundraising help churches today?

3. How is revival best defined? What is needed in order to see revival happen today?

4. Is revival mostly a sovereign act of God, the result of certain factors that we implement, or both? Why?

5. To what extent can revival be a natural and regular expression of New Testament Christianity? Are intensive short-term efforts at revitalization really preferable?

6. Do you think that the level of public response to past revival events, such as in Billy Graham's 1959 visit to Melbourne, could be achievable today? Why or why not?

7. Do any of the revival-hindering factors raised by Leonard Ravenhill adversely impact churches today? How might these and others realistically be combatted?

2.
Background to Revival

Early Churches in the City of Melbourne

The desire for pastoral expansion from the southern Australian state of Tasmania (Van Diemen's Land until 1856) led to the white settlement of Melbourne by John Batman in 1835. Batman sailed to Melbourne through Port Philip Bay and then along the Yarra River, famously stating upon his arrival: "This will be the place for a village."[1] His still-controversial purchase of 600,000 acres from the Indigenous inhabitants typified the many injustices perpetrated against Aboriginal people at the time,[2] but it nevertheless led to the establishment of a small settlement of wattle and daub huts, with 5,538 people and 925 houses in evidence by 1840.[3]

Early church services commenced in continuity with the worship practices of settlers. Wesleyan, Henry Reed, preached in Batman's home in an 1835 service attended by noted escaped convict, William Buckley.[4] The first regular minister, Reverend Joseph Orton, was another Wesleyan who commenced services in 1836, noting in a memorandum that he "took occasion to dwell on the propriety of a consistent deportment on the part of the settlers in this new settlement, particularly enjoining them to acknowledge God in all their ways."[5] The first church building in Melbourne was the

---

1. Grant and Serle, *The Melbourne Scene*, 4.
2. Harris, *One Blood*, 150. This sale was secured with various inexpensive items.
3. Selby, *The Memorial History*, 24.
4. Blamires and Smith, *The Early Story*, 13.
5. Grant and Serle, *The Melbourne Scene*, 24.

1837 Pioneers' Church of the Wesleyans[6] with the first Church of England (now Anglican) construction commencing in 1839.[7]

The discovery of gold in regional fields from 1851 saw the population expand significantly in Melbourne, the capital of the newly-independent colony of Victoria. The initial lack of clergy was quickly offset by continued government land grants to, and a subsidy of, Melbourne's churches.[8] Government aid, once it became proportionately allocated according to church affiliation reported in census figures, slowed the provision of education by the Wesleyan Methodists. With one fifth of the school population, despite having just one fourteenth of the general population, they had established 54 day-schools in Melbourne by 1856.[9]

Revivalism and Wesleyan Methodism

Although immigration resulted in the establishment of a variety of new churches and movements in Melbourne in the nineteenth century, the Wesleyan Methodists were sizeably represented and intensely evangelistic, growing from 5.5% of Victoria's population in 1841 to 10.7% in 1871[10] and then 15.0% by 1901.[11] Their first permanent church building was located in the township's soon-to-be-wealthy business district after acquisition of a £40 half-acre of land following forfeiture by a local speculator.[12]

The contribution of the Wesleyan Methodists to the evangelization of Melbourne in the nineteenth century was a substantial factor in shaping a revivalist climate of revitalizing fervor that led to Torrey's later visit to the city. Social impact, motivated by a holiness emphasis, included support for temperance and for restrictive gambling laws, but also included the establishment of various welfare initiatives. For example, when early growth had resulted in building debts in the 1850s, the Wesleyan Methodist Immigrants' Home was established. The provision of housing represented a joint concern for welfare and evangelism led by the colony's then chair of the Wesleyan Methodists. For Wesleyan minister, James Bickford, concerted

6. Piggin and Linder, *The Fountain of Public Prosperity*, 223.
7. Selby, *The Memorial History of Melbourne*, 159.
8. Grant and Serle, *The Melbourne Scene*, 81.
9. Blamires and Smith, *The Early Story*, 75–6.
10. Blamires and Smith, *The Early Story*, 315.
11. Coghlan, *Statistical Account 1901–1902*, 839.
12. Finn, *Chronicles*, 152.

evangelism was essential. Many had become "thoughtless of God and indifferent to the obligations of Church membership," and Melbourne was a "Babel of confusion and impiety."[13]

Early church expansion resulted from immigration, but also from the enthusiastic zeal of Wesleyan Methodist leaders. The new colony and township of Melbourne experienced growing numbers of church attendees through the efforts of many individual pioneer ministers. Despite not being in Melbourne any more than three years, William Schofield's ministry resulted in an increase of members from 181 in April 1843 to 360 in January 1846, and this included continued growth some months after his departure.[14] In 1838, a mere eighteen Wesleyan Methodists had been present in Melbourne.[15] By the time of Bickford's 1857 appointment to the regional goldfields town of Ballarat, almost twenty years later, that number had grown to 24,740 across the colony, being a five-fold increase on the Wesleyan population seen just six years prior.[16] It was noted that 4,000 could be found on the goldfields alone and that they became "a conserving element in the population there gathered."[17] Historian, Geoffrey Blainey, later reflected that the successful influence of Wesleyan Methodists at the time was due to a conviction that their work was important in connecting with the religious experiences of immigrants enjoyed prior to their departure from England. It also provided important connections in the face of newfound isolation.[18]

An 1854 Wesleyan Methodist district meeting proposed the building of new churches in inner Melbourne suburbs and the raising of £5,000 to open a grammar school (later known as Wesley College).[19] The effects of continued migration had necessitated the central church and land being sold for £40,000 to release funds for new buildings in the city and suburbs.[20] The first services in the new church (which still stands today) were

---

13. Bickford, *Christian Work*, 102.
14. Blamires and Smith, *The Early Story*, 40.
15. Bickford, *Christian Work*, 89.
16. Blamires and Smith, *The Early Story*, 315.
17. Blamires and Smith, *The Early Story*, 53.
18. Geoffrey Blainey, *The Heyday of the Churches*, 10–11.
19. Blamires and Smith, *The Early Story*, 66.
20. Blamires and Smith, *The Early Story*, 79; Finn, *Chronicles*, 152.

held in 1858. James Bickford proudly claimed some twenty years later that it ranked as "one of the finest ecclesiastical edifices" in Australia.[21]

The presence of numerous itinerant evangelists in the following decades continued this momentum, as did the impact of international revivals in the U.S.A. and Ireland which inspired evangelism by the members of the churches of greater Melbourne. On 22nd May 1859, the conversion of nine people led to daily services in suburban Brighton and neighbouring municipalities, with more than 100 people being added to the churches.[22] Numerous conversions resulted from two visits in the 1860s by William "California" Taylor (previously associated with ministry on Californian goldfields). The 1860s and 1870s ministry of Yorkshireman, Matthew Burnett, also contributed substantially to the expansion of the Methodist circuits across Melbourne and beyond.

The Wesleyan Methodists' work grew substantially and 480 churches were established by 1886, served by 109 ministers and 751 local preachers.[23] Despite increased ecumenical cooperation that would later become even more evident during the 1902 Mission, perhaps even foundational to its success, the *Southern Cross* quoted an influential minister lamenting in 1878 that there would be little likelihood of the Wesleyans merging with the other streams of Methodism active at the time.

> *I do not think the Wesleyan Methodist denomination is prepared to concede sufficient in order to obtain the union of the minor bodies. The Wesleyan view of the pastorate is so far removed from the practice which prevails in the other Methodist Churches that it seems morally impossible to bring the Methodists under one common government.*[24]

Unity with the Primitive Methodists, the Bible Christian Church, and the United Methodist Free Churches was nevertheless achieved in 1902, with the forming of the Methodist Church of Australasia just prior to the Melbourne Mission, after almost twenty years of discussion.[25] The union included 3,787 churches and 604,000 members (in an Australian population

---

21. Bickford, *Christian Work*, 111.
22. Blamires and Smith, *The Early Story*, 90–1.
23. Blamires and Smith, *The Early Story*, 314.
24. *Southern Cross*, 5th January 1878, 1.
25. *Age*, 1st January 1902, 5. The Methodist churches would later merge with the Congregational, and many Presbyterian, churches in 1977 to form the Uniting Church in Australia.

of almost 4 million).²⁶ The annual report of the united movement was eager to recognize "that the union of the four Methodist churches, hitherto separate – a union in which we all rejoice – [had] not been brought about without a considerable amount of prayer, Christian consideration and forbearance, and personal self-sacrifice."²⁷ In keeping with the spirit of such a commitment, then, the genuineness of sentiment concerning the Mission itself was heartfelt.

> We note with great thankfulness the great unanimity which prevails among the evangelical churches of Melbourne in promoting the forthcoming Simultaneous Mission, and especially that such thorough and widespread preparations are being made for it by the institution of a network of home prayer-meetings, touching thousands of homes, and extending over a continued period of time.²⁸

Evangelical Action and an Invitation to Spurgeon

Such cooperation was not new in Melbourne. In 1877, Henry Varley visited the city and preached in various locations, including to 7,000 at a Brighton picnic.²⁹ He had come on the invitation of the United Evangelistic Committee, known by mid-1878 as the United Evangelical Association (U.E.A.) which was established because of the alleged ineffectiveness of much evangelism in local churches.³⁰ Known locally due to his 1850s business interests, Varley had since returned to his London home. Now, various leading church representatives who were committed to inviting prominent evangelists to Melbourne were keen to see him return that the city might be transformed. During Varley's intervening ministry years in London, Charles Spurgeon invited him to preach in his famed Metropolitan Tabernacle. In addition, Varley participated in an all-night prayer service with Moody before famously remarking to him that the world was "yet to see what God can do with a man fully consecrated to Him."³¹ Varley contributed a five-month period of evangelistic ministry in Melbourne, drawing

---

26. *Southern Cross*, 10ᵗʰ January 1902, 43.
27. *Annual Pastoral Address 1902*, 150.
28. *Annual Pastoral Address 1902*, 154.
29. *Leader*, 10ᵗʰ November 1877, 20.
30. *Southern Cross*, 13ᵗʰ July 1878, 1.
31. Pollock, *Moody*, 96.

Background to Revival

sizeable crowds in the central Collins Street Baptist Church,[32] the city's Town Hall,[33] and various public spaces.[34]

The *Illustrated Australian News* noted that, although several preachers at the time had "devoted themselves ardently to the work of promoting a revival of Christian faith and practice," Henry Varley in particular was a revivalist "of considerable power and originality."[35] His impact was such that the *Southern Cross* observed there would be little fear of his converts standing the test if they would "only make use of their Bibles which he [made] of his."[36]

Writing in the *Ecclesiastical Observer* in 1878, James Hamill marveled at Varley's impact and observed that, in his prior experience of the preaching of both Alexander Somerville and Charles Spurgeon, he did not hear "the same critical grasp of Holy Scripture" as that which Varley demonstrated.[37] Hamill was no ordinary observer. As an evangelist engaged by the first Disciples of Christ church in Melbourne, he pioneered one of the largest of Melbourne's descendant Churches of Christ congregations in the outer south-eastern township of Berwick in 1869. Ninety years later a Hollywood movie about the end of the world was filmed both in Berwick and the greater city of Melbourne, being referenced in one of the Melbourne sermons delivered by Billy Graham whose visit coincided with filming.[38]

The non-denominational emphases of the Disciples at the time resonated with Varley who had assisted their development in Britain. It also resonated with the *Southern Cross* who opposed the involvement of some of "the more notable" representatives of the Plymouth Brethren at a baptism by Varley of more than a hundred people (attended by some fifteen hundred) advising that, "as long as he unduly favors any one denomination, [Varley] loses power with all the others in proportion."[39] One reader of the *Southern*

---

32. *Age*, 7th August 1877, 3.
33. *Weekly Times*, 18th August 1877, 14.
34. *Illustrated Australian News*, 3rd October 1877, 154.
35. *Illustrated Australian News*, 3rd October 1877, 154.
36. *Southern Cross*, 19th January 1878, 1.
37. *Ecclesiastical Observer*, 1st April 1878, 97. Hamill heard Spurgeon prior to relocating to Australia in 1867. Dr. Alexander Somerville, later the moderator of the Free Church of Scotland, visited Australia in 1877–78 and addressed large crowds of three to six thousand.
38. Graham, "The Second Coming," recorded February 1959 in Melbourne. The film, *On the Beach*, was based on a 1957 novel of the same name.
39. *Southern Cross*, 19th January 1878, 1.

Cross, also opposed to aspects of the public baptism, nevertheless affirmed Varley as an "unsectarian evangelist" which had meant that "ministers of various denominations rallied around him, thus giving to his meetings a status and an influence not otherwise possible."[40] The importance of Varley's ecumenical influence in his Melbourne Town Hall services undoubtedly inspired later cooperation seen in the 1902 Simultaneous Mission.

By 1881, and therefore twenty-one years before becoming a reality, the U.E.A. established a committee to investigate the possibility of a month-long mission in the city of Melbourne.[41] When the Association then failed in its attempt to secure a visit from one of its generation's most prominent evangelicals, the *Southern Cross* was inclined to report on the matter, publishing the letter declining the offer made to none other than Charles Spurgeon.

Upper Norwood, 9th May 1881

Dear Friends,

I thank you with all my heart for your warm-hearted invitation to Melbourne, but at the present I have no thought of leaving home. A voyage to Australia was, I believe spoken of, but I never seriously thought of it.

I should need a year or two to prepare for such a trip. The weekly sermon would need to be published, and therefore would need to be ready for the printer and this alone would involve an extra toil, for which I have no time or strength. The same is true in a smaller degree with the magazine.

You rightly mention the difficulty of the finances for my Institution. This is a very great one; indeed it is insuperable.

All things considered, you must regard me as chained to the oar, to live and die at my work, with such brief relaxations as I can find near home.

Should, however, my health fail me still more seriously, it will be a great comfort to know that there are friends in the southern seas who will welcome a broken-down soldier.

40. *Southern Cross*, 9th February 1878, 3.
41. *Southern Cross*, 27th August 1881, 1.

God bless you evermore and reward you for your generous feeling towards me.

Yours very heartily,

C. H. Spurgeon.[42]

Rather than pinning their hopes solely upon securing a keynote speaker of international renown, there was also growing recognition among Melbourne's evangelical leaders that other factors were essential, including a recognition that the gift of God would "honor the faithful endeavors of ordinary men and ministers."[43] Importantly, too, systematic action would be needed, the sort later adopted by the Simultaneous Mission but also seen in the activities of the Centennial Mission of 1888, held in acknowledgment of the nation's first white settlement one hundred years prior. Of the preparations made on that occasion it was remarked: "Never was so vast a proportion of the homes of Melbourne visited by the messengers of peace."[44] Far from holding any view that unity would "impair individual church action," a united evangelistic movement such as the U.E.A. could engage in work that was a much-needed feeder to the churches. The following comments were made regarding this need at its 1878 inception.

> *We should have been glad if the various churches had seen their way to have combined to carry out Christian work on the territorial system. In this way a more complete and systematic visitation of every lane, alley, court, and house would have been secured. We regret that the churches did not, long ago, take such a step; for on them, evidently, the responsibility rested of missioning the whole of Melbourne. Had they fulfilled their duty, no need whatever would have existed for launching forth a fresh Christian enterprise. Unfortunately, however, there is need for such an organization as the United Evangelistic Association with the platform which it provides for combined church action.*[45]

Later efforts at persistent prayer for evangelistic impact would be led by Melbourne minister, John MacNeil, who intentionally engaged in

---

42. *Southern Cross*, 27th August 1881, 1.
43. *Southern Cross*, 30th April 1881, 2.
44. *Southern Cross*, 28th December 1888, 1031.
45. *Southern Cross*, 20th July 1878, 2.

mission-focused services in suburban locations. MacNeil's fervency and effectiveness as an evangelist were affirmed by the *Southern Cross*.

> "Certainly he does not spare himself, but his reward will be given him. It is premature to speak of results, but appearances suggest that the spiritual life of believers is being deepened . . ."[46]

A Gathering Momentum – The Evangelization Society and D. L. Moody

Under the auspices of the U.E.A., a series of special Melbourne services was conducted in a 'Gospel Tent' by two evangelists in 1881, where the notion was sown that those invited could potentially be more comfortable in a marquee than in a place of worship.[47] Other such characteristics of the later Simultaneous Mission were typically associated with the culture of late nineteenth century evangelicalism.

> *The methods employed in 'revival meetings,' and, what is more noteworthy still, the theology of 'revival' teaching of all the churches, are almost identical. Singing of the fervent emotional type, pointed, ardent, and simple addresses, and the demand for instant decision, a decision to be declared by coming to the 'penitent form,' or the 'inquiry room,' are the features common to all their services. And no matter to what doctrinal or ecclesiastical school the revivalist or missioner belongs, the theology of all revival addresses is of precisely the same type: simple, orthodox, evangelical, unvexed by metaphysics, untroubled by doubt, and surcharged with Christ.*[48]

The U.E.A. ultimately failed to gain traction. With the assistance of Christian politician, James Balfour, and the provision of extra finance, many of the members wasted little time forming a new group in 1883, the Evangelization Society of Victoria (E.S.V.). It conducted regular evangelistic services, its restless determination to succeed in securing conversions becoming evident in a desire to address five stated distinctives.

1. *Man's sinful and lost condition through Adam's fall and his own personal sin.*

---

46. *Southern Cross*, 25th June 1881, 1. Also, services were later conducted in Prahran, Toorak, Armadale and Geelong (*Southern Cross*, 12th May 1883, 6).
47. *Southern Cross*, 30th April 1881, 1.
48. *Southern Cross*, 30th April 1881, 2.

2. *The salvation God has provided by the sacrifice of the Lord Jesus Christ, who by His death on the cross made atonement for sin.*
3. *The way in which we obtain this salvation – viz. by faith.*
4. *The changed life which is the fruit and consequence of faith.*
5. *The responsibility of all who hear this message.*[49]

Formed along the lines of the Evangelization Society of London, the E.S.V. drew leaders from multiple denominations. It also worked with representatives of the Young Men's Christian Association (Y.M.C.A.) in Melbourne in an attempt to deploy evangelists in towns across the colony. The establishment of the E.S.V. was rewarded with the rapid organization of some 500 evangelistic meetings in 30 townships. A subsequent pledge was made to seek a visit from Moody, being the most prominent evangelist in the world at the time.[50] The *Weekly Times* reported on evangelistic progress soon after the formation of the E.S.V.

> We are in possession of the first "Occasional Report" of the Evangelization Society of Victoria. After referring to the hearty welcome which the society received from Christians of all denominations since its inauguration three months ago, it narrates the successful work which has been prosecuted at Castlemaine, Walmer, Sandridge (Port Melbourne), Richmond, Williamstown, East Richmond, Mornington, Dromana, Barnes, Cowes, Frankston, Balnarring and Hastings; and to the meetings being held at Chewton and Lara. It then proceeds, "Arrangements have been made for services that will occupy the evangelists engaged for some months to come, while applications are constantly coming in. We have two evangelists entirely engaged in the work, two others who have been partially employed. We have also a goodly list of volunteers, who can occasionally take meetings."[51]

Balfour, on behalf of the E.S.V., met with Moody in Edinburgh in 1892 and urged him to come to Australia with his musical accompanist, Ira Sankey. In his correspondence with his colleagues at home he asked them to intercede: "Pray for [Moody's] coming; this is the best means to use. If it is God's will and for His glory, he will give us our request. Mr. Sankey is quite

---

49. Supplement to *Southern Cross*, 28th July 1883, 1–2.
50. *Age*, 19th February 1884, 5.
51. *Weekly Times*, 20th October 1883, 6.

prepared to accompany him."[52] In reporting on the matter, the *Southern Cross* also noted that recent services coordinated by the E.S.V. had totalled a sizeable 139 for the month of November with 9,624 people in attendance.[53] Meticulous attention was given to the recording of numerical attendances and to the outcomes of evangelistic appeals seen in services at that time. It accompanied the belief that consolidating *decisions* to follow Christ was crucial for the subsequent formation of new *disciples*.

The *Southern Cross* subsequently published news of the formal request sent to Moody and Sankey by the E.S.V. It had been accompanied by a lengthy petition coming from a wide range of churches and represented the pinnacle of the efforts of the E.S.V. to date.

> *Dear Sir, - By this mail we are forwarding to our beloved brethren, Messrs. Moody and Sankey, the invitation which the executive were requested to prepare, urging them if possible to visit Australia.*
>
> *The response to the circular which was sent to the various churches in the colony, to be signed by the ministers and Christian workers, has been very hearty and general, showing the deepest sympathy and readiness to help in every way, should these servants of Christ be directed by the Master to accept of [sic.] this invitation.*
>
> *The petition is signed by 1,384 persons, representing 229 churches.*
>
> *It now remains for those who are interested in evangelistic work to wait much on God in fervent prayer, that the right decision may be made, and the will of the Lord. be done. – Yours sincerely, Chas. Carter, Secretary.*[54]

Several months later, an update to readers of the *Southern Cross* revealed the deflating news that commitments in Norway, Sweden and England were to be followed by a series of evangelistic events in Chicago, making a visit to Australia impossible in the near future.[55]

When a further attempt was made to secure Moody for the long-awaited month of mission services in Melbourne, the churches secured far broader support. The E.S.V. had become the Evangelization Society of Australasia (E.S.A.) in 1896 as its work spread to other Australian colonies.

52. *Southern Cross*, 8th January 1892, 35.
53. *Southern Cross*, 8th January 1892, 35.
54. *Southern Cross*, 19th February 1892, 155.
55. *Southern Cross*, 13th May 1892, 386.

Background to Revival

The *Southern Cross* revealed a desire for every evangelical church to issue a request in services on Sunday 25th September 1898 for congregation members to sign a petition and to return their papers to the Evangelization Society by 9th October.[56] Assistance was sought from each Australian colony to ensure widespread representation. The letter to Moody which accompanied the amassed petition revealed an understanding of the need for an experiential faith distinct from formalized religious observance, as was commonly evident in the evangelical churches. The letter was published in the *Southern Cross*.

> Dear Sir,
>
> On behalf of many evangelical Christians in Australasia and New Zealand, we address you, with the request that you come to these lands also with that Gospel message which you have been enabled to publish in so many other places with demonstration of the Spirit and with power.
>
> There are nearly four millions of people in these colonies speaking the English tongue, and almost all of them of the Anglo-Saxon race; our largest cities containing from 3,000 to 400,000 inhabitants. Christian ordinances are widely established among us, and the outward observances of religion are well attended to; but it is felt by us that the ordinary means of grace would have increased influence if the stimulus of a fresh statement of the glorious Gospel were made to multitudes who have already heard it preached, without as yet having felt its power.
>
> The necessary expenses attending such a visit have been virtually arranged for, and if you see your way to comply with our request the cost of your passage will at once be remitted.
>
> We are aware that this is not the first similar request that you have had from Australia, and that you have not hitherto been led to comply; but we would point out to you that the present invitation comes with a united voice from all the colonies, and from all evangelical denominations, and would assure you that it is accompanied by many prayers to God, that His Spirit may lead you here, and make your coming the means of widespread blessing.[57]

---

56. *Southern Cross*, 16th September 1898, 894.
57. *Southern Cross*, 16th September 1898, 894.

Global Revival

The *Southern Cross* advised its readers of the completion of the petition. With 6,538 signatures from 196 Victorian churches, and 15,831 signatures from 454 churches in total, inclusive of 87 churches in New Zealand, the petition was sent to Moody in bound form "to impress him."[58] By April the following year, the *Southern Cross* was able to publish the reply from Moody, addressed to the secretary of the Evangelization Society of Australasia.

> *My Dear Mr. Carter,*
>
> *It is with a very deep sense of appreciation that I acknowledge the cordial invitation extended by the Evangelization Society of Australasia to visit the cities of New Zealand and Australia, and were my own personal pleasure to be consulted I would at once have cabled my acceptance. It is a privilege to work and meet with fellow labourers in the Master's service in different quarters of the globe, and I know that there would be real joy in the association of such a mission as you invite me to conduct under your auspices in Australasia.*
>
> *There are several obstacles, however, that seem to me to be insurmountable, and on that account I must take it to be God's purpose for me to remain in America for the present. Within the past twenty years I have been led and enabled to establish three schools, which have steadily increased in size, and now have over a thousand students enrolled. These schools alone are an important part of my life work, and I feel that I am increasingly needed in their administration and care. There is never a day but that I am in communication with the various heads of the departments, and I feel that I am needed still in the development of the work inaugurated.*
>
> *The conditions in my own country also make it hard to leave for work elsewhere. Never have I received such hearty support from churches and ministers in this country as of recent years, and this I believe to be the very call of God for greater labour and activity where He is opening the way. This past year I believe to be the best year of my life, and the work that God has accomplished this year so far promises to make 1899 better than any year in the past.*
>
> *Still another objection to accepting this invitation is in the advice of my doctors to avoid a long and especially a warm ocean voyage. A few years ago I planned to visit India and China in a trip around the world but was obliged to give it up on the urgent counsel of friends.*

---

58. *Southern Cross*, 30th December 1898, 1255.

Background to Revival

The long ocean voyage attended by tropical heat has been something that I have especially been warned against.

These are my chief obstacles to accepting the very cordial and hearty invitation which you extend in behalf of the Evangelization Society of Australasia, and I am led to believe that they are an evidence of God's purposes for me. I would thank you for the heartiness of your invitation, and for the warm, Christian fellowship which it expresses. We are, indeed, in one family, and with one Lord and Master labouring in a common cause, and although it may not be my privilege to meet and labour with the church in Australasia, I shall look forward with still greater expectancy to the privilege of doing so when there shall be 'no more sea.'

Yours in the Gospel,

D. L. Moody.[59]

The *Southern Cross* reflected the prevailing disappointment concerning Moody's response, despite the continued desire of the Evangelization Society to pursue a significant mission in Melbourne. Its editorial in the following week's edition reflected a realistic appraisal of the situation: "Under the circumstances, no one would wish him to run the risk of coming to us, but there can be no doubt that it is a great loss to the Christianity of these colonies not to be stirred up and incited to more activity by so strong, so reasonable, and so spiritual a man."[60] As Moody's letter hinted, his health was deteriorating. Moody would pass away just eight months later.

Mission Central – A Passion for Evangelism

The late nineteenth century Church continued to see the rise of evangelical movements and missioners in Australia. Plans for a major event in Melbourne did not deter evangelical Christians from also organizing various other missions, particularly in the form of multi-day conventions with their many services and speakers. The rise of the Y.M.C.A. and the Christian Endeavor Movement, which was committed to the cultivation of spiritual growth among young people in Australia from 1883, were among these. The emergence of the Salvation Army in Victoria in 1882 was accompanied

---

59. *Southern Cross*, 21st April 1899, 374.
60. *Southern Cross*, 28th April 1899, 387.

by rapid growth through evangelism, with 137 ministry leaders state-wide in 1887[61] growing to 368 by 1889[62] and 458 by 1891,[63] when the founding leader and 'general,' William Booth, visited Melbourne.[64] One particular address was given which the *Southern Cross* believed to contain as much "practical sagacity and true statesmanship as his Christian philanthropy," with Booth being "no weak sentimentalist or dreaming theorist, but an intensely practical common-sense man," demonstrating an intelligence penetrating "beneath all surface facts to the underlying moral causes."[65] The Christianity of this period sought to be *trans*-formative, not simply *in*-formative. Evangelistic work could not hope to impact the human spirit unless it also revealed its revivalistic soul.

That soul was evidenced not only in the impact of evangelism on society, but also on revitalization of the Church. A call to holiness typically sought to mobilize the evangelistic impetus of churches in sessions at public ministry conventions, but it also grew strongly through continued Wesleyan Methodist influences and through the emergence of the Keswick movement. Originating in Britain, it established an 1891 holiness convention in the city of Geelong, near Melbourne, utilizing the visiting evangelist, George Grubb. Grubb preached in many Melbourne congregations of the Episcopal (Anglican) Church that had been strongly associated with the Keswick movement. Many Keswick speakers were Wesleyan Methodists and the coalescing of Keswick and Wesleyan Methodist holiness emphases significantly and positively influenced the evangelistic climate within which Torrey was ultimately brought to Melbourne.[66]

Learning from Others - 1901

The inspiration for the format used in the eventual mission in Melbourne was, in part, the similar mission held in Sydney in November of 1901. It likewise followed a familiar and thorough organizational pattern that had been used in other missions held internationally. John Watsford, a long-term Methodist and key organizer of the Sydney event, spoke of its

---

61. Hayter, *Victorian Year Book 1887–1888*, 46.
62. Hayter, *Victorian Year Book 1889–1890*, 371.
63. Hayter, *Victorian Year Book 1892*, 366.
64. Jupp, "Salvationists," 557.
65. *Southern Cross*, 2nd October 1891, 783.
66. Evans, *Evangelism and Revivals*, 64.

glorious success in bringing the conversions of more than three thousand people.[67] A letter co-signed by the Sydney organizers was published in a major daily newspaper before the event's commencement. It indicated that at least thirty districts would participate voluntarily and would coordinate and finance their own local missions without a general appeal being made for funding. The districts were served by volunteer workers who went from house to house, inviting all to attend the meetings. The Simultaneous Mission of Sydney used multiple churches, halls, and tents as venues, replicating the methodology adopted throughout England that same year. The Sydney event saw those responding to sermons spoken to in "inquiry rooms," which were established for the purpose of securing commitments to follow Christ.[68]

The *Southern Cross* detailed the lessons learned from the Sydney event and created a central management committee to consist of six persons supported by various other committees responsible for: (1) prayer meetings; (2) literature and hymn books (selling for a half penny); (3) the selection of missioners; (4) finance; (5) venues; (6) children's services; and (7) press and advertising. There was door-to-door visitation, the use of tents and public halls, and the adoption of prayer and mission strategies affirmed by international evangelists.[69] Sydney had noted the priority of organization, preparation, and unity, and Melbourne would accentuate the importance of each dimension in delivering more than double the number converts.[70]

The *Southern Cross* proudly noted the involvement of every Evangelical denomination in Melbourne.[71] During the mission, intense daily schedules were to include 7 a.m. prayer meetings, "midday services at noon for businessmen," 3 p.m. Bible reading meetings, and 8 p.m. evangelistic services. Such was the effort expended in Melbourne, that the Methodist *Spectator* confidently remarked: "Never before has such a stupendous work been undertaken in the religious interest of Australian people."[72] The *Missionary Review of the World* would similarly reflect on the significance of the Mission, suggesting it ultimately produced "results seldom seen in any

---

67. *Southern Cross*, 20th December 1901, 1410.
68. *Southern Cross*, 20th December 1901, 1410.
69. *Sydney Morning Herald*, 27th September 1901, 4.
70. *Australian Town and Country Journal*, 7th December 1901, 11.
71. *Southern Cross*, 10th January 1902, 87.
72. *Spectator*, 18th April 1902, 555.

century."[73] Such outcomes were dependent in no small way upon the preparations being made for revival.

Study Questions

1. What factors led to the proportion of Wesleyan Methodists almost tripling in Melbourne between 1841 and 1901? Could such growth be achievable again?

2. What do you think of the Wesleyan Methodists' balance between evangelism and social justice in the nineteenth century? How might churches learn from this today?

3. What do you notice about the letters from Charles Spurgeon and D. L. Moody declining their invitations to speak in Melbourne? Why is it seemingly important to have well-known figures leading prominent events still today?

4. What do you think of the purpose statement of the Evangelization Society of Victoria? Would it be a help or a hindrance to guiding evangelism today?

5. How would you evaluate the use of a petition such as the one presented to Moody? Do petitions (even by means of social media) serve a helpful purpose for churches today?

6. The holiness emphasis of late nineteenth century movements saw opposition to dancing, smoking, gambling, and the sale and consumption of alcohol. Were such behavioural expectations any more or less reasonable in an era where most people had a Christian heritage? What should holiness look like today?

7. The Melbourne filming of a movie about the world's end – On The Beach – coincided with Billy Graham's 1959 visit to the city. Why would he have referenced it in an evangelistic sermon? How are such cultural references useful today?

---

73. *Missionary Review* 1902, 779.

3.
Preparations for Revival

Human Effort or Divine Sovereignty?

The idea that a spiritual awakening, or revival, may emerge from intentional activity or systematic processes seems to suggest prioritizing human effort over the sovereignty of God. As mentioned in Chapter 1, both elements are required, just as they were in 1902 when creating contexts for prolonged prayer and diligent ecumenical cooperation cultivated spiritual vitality, one of the four essential keys to revival. For the organizers, then, the overall event would necessarily become infused with divine potential. The *Southern Cross* clarified the balance.

> The Simultaneous Mission merely supplies the human conditions – of faith, of sacrifice, of toil, of spiritual expectation – through which the divine and ever-working Spirit of God reaches the end sought by His grace.[1]

Divine inspiration for, and activation of, the Mission was strongly desired in Melbourne at the time. Perhaps one major daily newspaper's error was Freudian when mistakenly referring to the second keynote speaker, William Edgar Geil, as Edgar 'Zeal' early in 1902.[2] The Rev. J. P. McCann opened a briefing meeting concerning the Mission, and summed up the anticipation in his prayer: "Lord, we are expecting great things."[3] Torrey himself was more explicit, stating: "I believe we are on the eve of one of the

---

1. *Southern Cross*, 7th February 1902, 155.
2. *Argus*, 10th February 1902, 4.
3. *Southern Cross*, 31st January 1902, 131.

greatest religious awakenings throughout the whole earth which has ever been seen."[4] To what extent could that genuinely be true? What would have inspired such confidence?

Geil's Methodology

Though in earnest preparations for the approaching Melbourne mission, Carey was keen to assist his northern counterparts. Geil, due to speak in Melbourne while on his self-funded global mission travels, was rushed to Sydney to assist their own revival meetings. Geil was considered by Y.M.C.A. general secretary, John J. Virgo, to be the "one of the foremost lay preachers in America."[5] With "no time to implement his preparatory method," though, he was unable to "render Sydney the full measure of his experience and strength."[6]

Did Geil possess a methodology truly critical to a unique level of success in Melbourne? The *Southern Cross* explained that, while people were converted in Sydney, people *and* churches were converted in Melbourne. While Sydney's impact was limited, Melbourne's was "sweeping right through the state."[7] Indeed, seven weeks of two thousand home prayer meetings had been advocated by Geil in Melbourne, whereas Sydney was unable to utilize organized prayer to this extent. While the *Spectator* encouraged the work of prayer to be done "as far as possible, anonymously,"[8] Carey sought to highlight the impact of Melbourne's prayer circles.

> It is impossible to express the new life and the deep joy that came to the churches through these quiet home meetings. Homes that had never dreamed of such a service were flung open; not just the homes of the poor, but of the rich. Men who had never conducted public prayer made the venture, and before the seven weeks were over were enthusiastic in their new work . . . One church in the suburbs had more than thirty home prayer meetings running. We heard of streets where passers-by on those Tuesday evenings were made to wonder what was happening as they caught from house to house the strains of our preparatory hymns. In several instances men and women

---

4. *Leader*, 12th April 1902, 25.
5. Virgo, *Fifty Years*, 66.
6. Carey, "Conspiracy of Circumstances," 249.
7. *Southern Cross*, 23rd May 1902, 620.
8. *Spectator*, 14th February 1902, 224.

Preparations for Revival

attending the home meetings, under the influence of their holy quiet, gave their hearts for the first time to God.[9]

There were, however, multiple coalescing factors in Melbourne's impact. Its event was preceded by multiple prior years of prayer, both in the city and abroad. It also demonstrated a clear synergy resulting from the featuring of three international guests who had been involved in the Simultaneous Mission services that immediately preceded the central gatherings. Undoubtedly, the contributions by Torrey and Alexander to the Mission complemented Geil's stylistic difference. Also, 30,000 'Get Right with God' cards were printed by a friend of Alexander's and crowds were encouraged to "sow the town with them."[10] Prior to the commencement of the Melbourne Mission, too, seventy ministers had been asked to help at the various local mission venues where prayer teams were being organized around designated prayer captains. Additionally, a prayer meeting committee was organized for Melbourne and initiated a series of one-hour 3pm Monday devotional prayer meetings for ministers.[11] It seemed multiple streams of prayer and planning were indeed converging upon the river of evangelistic impact that eventually flowed with force.

Geil was evidently an important voice, giving clarity to the preparation and the mobilization of the home prayer meetings. He believed that most missions tended to falter for lack of sufficient preparation or church involvement. His idealized plan was therefore presented to, and implemented by, the Melbourne organizers, and was summarized by Carey.

> *Get every church that joins in any mission to appoint a chief leader – the strongest, most magnetic member of that church. He, with the pastor, must discover and appoint a score of the best men in the church to be leaders of a series of home prayer meetings. He, with the pastor, must also persuade a score of Christian householders to open their homes for the welcome of these meetings. Some eight or ten persons should attend each meeting in each house. For seven successive weeks before the mission in each of these homes on the same evening of the week these prayer circles should meet. A leader's handbook should be prepared, giving the exact order which such prayer meetings should take, fixing the hymns to be sung, the scriptures to be read, and the topics for the brief exhortations. The topics ought to lead up by wise gradation to the Mission, e.g. (1) prayer, (2) work,*

---

9. Carey, "Conspiracy of Circumstances," 253.
10. Williamson, *A Great Revival*, 34.
11. *Spectator*, 28th February 1902, 293.

(3) work here, (4) work now, (5) work gives joy, (6) the promise to the worker, (7) the power of the Spirit. Encourage everybody in each home to offer audible prayer. Now imagine 100 churches joining in such a mission in your city and carrying through this programme. Don't you see that you get 2,000 prayer meetings a week, and 20,000 people on their knees at the same hour of the week, for seven successive weeks on behalf of the mission? Think of that. In response to such massive entreaty what downpours of blessing would be sure to fall![12]

Notwithstanding the intentionality of preparation, revival historian, J. Edwin Orr, indeed sees Melbourne's mission as a culmination of earlier revival efforts, but one that provided an evolving awakening that resulted from concerted prayer.[13] It will also be shown in Chapter 7 that significant and subsequent global revival phenomena observed early in the twentieth century were linked to Australia through this particular Simultaneous Mission and that the foundation to its success, a success replicable in England, Wales, and India, for example, was unprecedented prayer in a spirit of unity.

Securing Torrey

At the close of a week of prayer in Chicago in 1898, a woman inspired a group to meet weekly to pray for revival. A one-hour gathering commenced on Tuesdays before shifting to Saturday evenings, either in Torrey's home or in the Bible Institute after classes had concluded.[14] An average of 300 people attended and a second, longer meeting soon began to be held until 2 a.m. on Sunday mornings, in keeping with Torrey's motto, 'pray through.'[15] At one such meeting, one of the leaders prayed that Torrey himself would be sent around the world to preach the Gospel and this immediately resonated with him.[16] Torrey began to pray that God would send him across the world to see thousands of conversions in China, Japan, Australia, New Zealand, India, Germany and Great Britain. Later, the Australian pianist for Torrey's meetings, Robert Harkness, noted that Torrey "was quite outside himself as he prayed, borne along by the Holy Spirit."[17] After the Melbourne Mission, Torrey recalled that his prayer had been, "send me round

12. Carey, "Conspiracy of Circumstances," 246–7.
13. Orr, *Evangelical Awakenings*, 105.
14. *Southern Cross*, 27th February 1903, 210; Harkness, *The Man*, 19.
15. Davis, *Torrey and Alexander*, 11–12.
16. Davis, *Torrey and Alexander*, 12.
17. Harkness, *The Man*, 19.

Preparations for Revival

the world, preaching the Gospel, and to see thousands of souls converted to the Gospel of the Son of God."[18]

Unclear as to how he might carry out his local duties and this new responsibility he resolved to trust that the God of the call would provide the means to its fulfilment. The visit of William Warren and G. P. Barber on behalf of the churches of Melbourne soon after resulted in them asking him to front their Simultaneous Mission there in 1902. Torrey responded by indicating he would commit the matter to prayer and "leave God to decide."[19]

Torrey's account reveals he had experienced a reluctance to abandon the Bible Institute and the Chicago Avenue Church (later known as 'The Moody Church') when considering his travels. His duties had preoccupied him extensively following Moody's death in 1899. It was several months later that Torrey received a cabled request to accept his invitation to Australia with the promise of money to fund the journey. After further prayer, Torrey finally indicated that "God made it clear that [he] should go."[20]

The Australian churches suggested an accompanying singer and Torrey settled on Charles Alexander, being a former student of the Moody Bible Institute. His passage to Melbourne was secured with a long-distance call.[21] Believing he would arrive there before Alexander, Torrey neglected to mention his decision to appoint Alexander to the organizing committee. J. J. Virgo, who had already been rehearsing with the choir soon met Alexander who appeared in Melbourne and learned of his understanding. Alexander claimed he had been told no-one could sing gospel songs in Australia, let alone amass a large choir. Virgo's response? "Everyone sings here except my eldest brother."[22] The two men connected immediately, and Virgo proposed to the event organizers that he relinquish most of his own role in order to accommodate Alexander.[23]

Against the seemingly clear sense of call to respond to the request by Warren and Barber was the simmering tension between Torrey and the trustees of the Institute on the matter of divine healing, just as there had been (privately) between Torrey and Moody before the latter's death.[24] This situation will be further explored in the next chapter. The opportunity to

18. *Southern Cross*, 27th February 1903, 210.
19. Harkness, *The Man*, 19; Warren, "Genesis," 202.
20. Torrey, *The Power of Prayer*, 48.
21. Davis, *Torrey and Alexander*, 13.
22. Virgo, *Fifty Years*, 67.
23. Alexander, *A Romance*, 50.
24. Gloege, *Guaranteed Pure*, 110–1, 122–3.

take a leave of absence from Chicago was both timely and fortuitous, an assessment later underscored by the stunning success of the Melbourne visit.

Charles Carter, as secretary of the Evangelization Society of Australasia,[25] must have felt a great sense of relief when writing of the securing of Torrey after his predecessor's inability to come to Melbourne. The *Southern Cross* reported his notification, inclusive of a claim that Moody had remarked to Torrey: "If I were you, I should take a preaching tour through Japan, China and Australia."[26] It went on to record Torrey's correspondence to the organizers, hinting at his belief that the Chicago prayers would be answered with global impact.

> *Now about the meetings in Australia. It is impossible to move a great city in a week or two, and produce satisfactory results. If we can stir one city, the fire will spread to smaller ones. As a general plan of campaign, I should expect to preach in the evening to the unsaved; in the afternoon to have a systematic course of Bible teaching on the great fundamental doctrines, including such subjects as prayer, the present work of the Holy Spirit, the Atonement, etc. I think it would be well also to have meetings for the children. I do not know that I should be able to conduct very many of these personally; but Mrs Torrey would help in them, and could conduct wherever necessary. I wish we also might have a prayer-meeting every day. We can expect no satisfactory and permanent results unless there is a great deal of prayer among the people. We are praying and expecting that the whole country will be moved.*
>
> *God is wonderfully blessing us at the church at this present time and in the Institute. Last Sunday was a day of great power. Many Christians came out into a deeper experience of God's grace, and many unsaved ones were brought to Christ.*
>
> *I will let you know as soon as possible the exact date of my arrival in Melbourne. Of course, we shall want to begin work at once.*
>
> *R. A. Torrey*[27]

---

25. The Evangelization Society of Victoria was renamed the Evangelization Society of Australasia in 1896 as the work began to broaden into other colonies. By 1901, when the colonies became states, the evangelistic effort also included New Zealand.

26. *Southern Cross*, 20th December 1901, 1410.

27. *Southern Cross*, 20th December 1901, 1410.

Preparations for Revival

Torrey's wife, Clara, travelled with him. Her diary of the tour, affectionately referencing her husband as 'Archie,' revealed him to be "the dearest man," and it clearly affirmed her admiration of her husband: "The Lord has certainly been good to me in giving me such a good, strong helper."[28] The diary also showed Clara Torrey's ministry interest through her "great joy of leading a young girl to Christ," and later acknowledged that Melbourne had been "wakened" through the Simultaneous Mission. It also revealed the difficult reality of an extended separation from the couple's children: "This morning brought the U.S. mail, three letters from each of the children . . . The children keep well. I praise God for all His goodness to us." The diary also recorded Clara's gratitude for the gifts presented by the organizers of the Mission on its last evening which included a gold watch and chain for her husband, and a "very pretty pearl crescent" for herself.[29]

The 'Prayer Band'

Robert Harkness assessed that prayer was a "natural exercise" for Torrey, "a real transaction with God," so that "every detail of his life" was committed to "frequent prayer."[30] In addition to Torrey's Chicago prayer meetings, though, extensive prayer efforts had been continuing in Melbourne for many years.

In his extensive coverage of Australian revivals before and after the 1902 Mission, Robert Evans observes that these revival foundations of prayer that were typically attributed to evangelist, John MacNeil, may have overlooked other significant national contributors to the prevailing religious mood.[31] Evans identifies the widespread impact of individuals such as the evangelist, Margaret Hampson, whose missions and Women's Prayer Unions were established in towns and churches across Australia and New Zealand in the 1880s.[32] The rise of various examples of prayer unions committed to intercession for revival also contributed to the increased spiritual fervor observed nationally at the time.[33] Similarly, the Christian Endeavor Movement grew quickly, with 3,000 members in Victoria in 1891 and

---

28. Clara Torrey, Diary, 23rd June 1902.
29. Clara Torrey, Diary, 23rd June 1902.
30. Harkness, *The Man*, 24.
31. Evans, *Evangelism and Revivals*, 3–4.
32. Evans, *Evangelism and Revivals*, 22–63.
33. Evans, *Evangelism and Revivals*, 9.

8,000 just a year later.[34] This group claimed more than 50,000 members Australia-wide by 1897 and was assessed by the *Missionary Review of the World* as the most strongly-entrenched example of the movement globally, and "one of the most remarkable developments in [then] current religious life."[35] Evans asserts that "it would be hard to overestimate the value of the contribution this movement made to the spiritual life of the period, as expressed in the evangelical Protestant churches in Australia."[36]

These initiatives, though indeed important in helping to stimulate a desire for revival in Melbourne, were less focused on uniting diverse groups of Christians in specific and local prayer. It was the more ecumenical efforts of this type that ultimately galvanised various groups committed to evangelization within the city. William Warren identified Melbourne-based activities such as a monthly Prayer Union, noting furthermore that thirty of the 1902 prayer circles were started by his wife,[37] however he also acknowledged the great significance of the work of MacNeil's "Band of Prayer" in engaging in concerted intercession from 1889.[38]

MacNeil initially sought one day of prayer which he called for the Presbyterian Church of Victoria, although he also rallied ministers from other Christian denominations to join him.

> *Why should not all the churches, indeed, join in one great league for prayer? The Baptist churches of Melbourne are giving themselves to united application with great devotion and fervor, and the infection of that noble example ought to run through all the denominations. There is stern need for prayer, for evil is strong, and sin spreads, and men are perishing, and Christ is dishonored. And there is ample encouragement to prayer.*[39]

The day itself was advertised in *The Age* newspaper, inclusive of the names of several ministers who later became synonymous with the 1902 Mission.

> *All Day of United Prayer for an outpouring of the Holy Spirit, Temperance Hall, Russell Street, 10 a.m. till 5pm and 7:30 p.m. till 10 p.m. Bring Bibles and Sankey's hymns. Chairmen: Revs. Macartney,*

---

34. Evans, *Evangelism and Revivals*, 173.
35. *Missionary Review* 1897, 314.
36. Evans, *Evangelism and Revivals*, 189.
37. Warren, "Genesis," 201.
38. Warren, "Genesis," 201.
39. *Southern Cross*, 23rd August 1889, 663.

Preparations for Revival

Rudduck, Crisp, Ewing, Webb, MacNeil, Chapman, Watsford, Langley.[40]

MacNeil's wife, in her 1897 biography of her then-late husband who died unexpectedly a year earlier, observed that the first "all-nights of prayer" on 14th August 1889 had led to the Day of Prayer and the formation of a group of ministers continuing to pray weekly for a "Great Revival." The interdenominational prayer group soon increased to almost forty participants. MacNeil's diary recorded the prayer day launch of what became known as his 'Prayer Band.'

> October 3rd, 1889, is over and gone – a day the like of which Melbourne has never seen. The results will be felt through Eternity. We sent a circular to every Minister in the Colony, asking them to fall in with us. At 10 a.m. we met in the Temperance Hall, an "upper room," and went on till 5, the attendance growing all day, till there must have been 700 present ere the afternoon closed.[41]

Though commencing under the leadership of MacNeil, the prayer meetings continued beyond his sudden 1896 death which was noted in local newspapers.[42] Twenty-three of the ministers who had prayed regularly with MacNeil corresponded with his wife to express their grief at his passing and their gratitude for his contribution (see Appendix 4).[43]

At one of the early 1902 Mission services, the Rev. W. Lockhart Morton of Adelaide recalled an early meeting, held at his home in Melbourne, in which evolved the phrase that later became synonymous with the Mission, "Lord, send the big revival." Morton, confident that this prayer was about to be answered, urged individual faith and the prayer of those same words.[44]

Coordinating Mission

W. H. Fitchett, president of the Methodist Conference and publisher of the *Southern Cross* newspaper, lauded three vital ingredients to the success of

---

40. *The Age*, 3rd October 1889, 1.
41. MacNeil, *John MacNeil*, 195–6.
42. *Port Melbourne Standard*, 29th August 1896, 2; *Williamstown Chronicle*, 29th August 1896, 2.
43. MacNeil, *John MacNeil*, 394–5.
44. *Southern Cross*, 18th April 1902, 433.

the Mission, being prayer, inter-church co-operation, and organization.[45] The significant coordinating role of the Mission's leaders (see Chapter 5) needs examination alongside consideration of its specific outcomes and the role of supporting individuals and church leaders in bringing individual impact. Torrey advocated as his prescription for revival that Christians surrender to God and pray with Holy Spirit earnestness. Any work of God was to be accomplished through the participation and commitment of church members. This work was explained by Geil with reference to his prayer methodology.

> *Most missions fail for lack of sufficient systematic, strenuous, spiritual preparation, and because the responsibility rests so unduly on the missioner and not on the churches; so that when the missioner vanishes, the influence of the mission also tends to pass away. That simply could not happen with a plan like mine.*[46]

In January 1902, the *Southern Cross* announced that the mission would commence on 13th April and that all evangelical churches and organizations were to be involved, with significant contributions needed from individuals. The home prayer circles were being formed at the time and choirs of fifty were being recruited for the preliminary local events.[47] It was claimed that "the whole of Greater Melbourne [had] been visited twice over from house to house with special invitations to the Mission."[48] It seemed no effort was spared as the organizers sought "to win hard-headed, vigorous-willed men" with methods they were confident would "prevail to achieve that end."[49] The object, then, was "to attract the notice of the man in the street, and urge upon him the claims of religion [in a] concerted attack by evangelistic workers upon the indifference of such a large proportion of the people to religious matters."[50]

Simultaneous meetings were to be held in the fifty allocated town halls and tents across a fortnight, with no meetings to be held in the city center during this two-week period. The *Southern Cross* proudly claimed that

---

45. Packer, "Revival No. 1," 264. Jabez Packer was a journalist with Sydney's *Daily Telegraph* who also founded the *Australian Baptist* newspaper.
46. Carey, "Conspiracy of Circumstances," 248.
47. *Southern Cross*, 28th March 1902, 353.
48. *Southern Cross*, 11th April 1902, 406; *Missionary Review* 1903, 202.
49. *Southern Cross*, 11th April 1902, 406.
50. *Argus*, 12th April 1902, 19.

Preparations for Revival

nearly half the halls of the city were in use.[51] Tents were preferred, where possible, as the Sydney mission had revealed 25% of attendees at tent missions were non-churchgoers, compared with 5% in halls, but a request had to be made for some of those very tents to be shipped to Melbourne due to an inadequate supply.[52] It was announced that, joining Torrey in the local events would be a range of missioners, including several American speakers, notably D. C. Davidson, and J. Lyall, as well as W. E. Geil.[53]

The event was being backed by several organizations. The Council of Churches in Melbourne (whose evangelistic committee was represented by Edward Harris) would join with the Evangelization Society of Australasia (led by Charles Carter), the Evangelical Churches Association (led by J. C. Langley), and the Y.M.C.A. (led by J. J. Virgo), who would all join Carey as Chairman and S. C. Kent as Vice-Chairman. The Melbourne City Mission, the Sunday School Union, and others would also assist, and denominational support would be secured. In all, seventy-six people were primarily involved in support of the central committee.[54] With 214 churches involved, unprecedented unity was on display unlike that seen in England's mission, especially in light of the inclusion of twenty-seven Anglican churches in Melbourne. These joined fifty-nine Methodist churches, forty Presbyterian churches, thirty-seven Baptist churches, twenty-six Congregational churches, one Lutheran church, and twenty-four Salvation Army corps.[55] The absence of personal or denominational interest was evidenced by the absence of friction throughout the coordination of the event.[56] Ministers marveled at the organization and unity demonstrated as churches worked together for "the salvation of souls."[57]

At the close of the four-week Mission, Geil would go on to claim: "The preparatory work was the best done of any that I know of, for a city of this size, in the history of the Christian Church," with the number of conversions being "stupendous."[58]

---

51. *Southern Cross*, 28th March 1902, 339.
52. *Southern Cross*, 28th March 1902, 353.
53. *Southern Cross*, 24th January 1902, 87.
54. *Weekly Times*, 19th April 1902, 13.
55. *Southern Cross*, 28th March 1902, 353.
56. Packer, "Revival No. 1," 260.
57. *Southern Cross*, 16th May 1902, 592.
58. *Southern Cross*, 30th May 1902, 656.

'Decision cards' were used in order to track commitments to faith in Christ. Recorded on these cards were the names of those affirming the following words.

> *The Acceptance of Christ: In humble reliance on the promises of God, and on the aid of the Holy Spirit, I do, here and now, accept Jesus Christ to be my Saviour and Lord, with full purpose of heart, to confess Him, and to follow and serve Him all my days.*[59]

Torrey would typically ask converts to make a profession of faith, usually by standing in response to an invitation to commit to Christ.

> *People who want to be Christians ought to be ready to get up and make a definite acknowledgment of the fact. I do not say, of course, that a man cannot be saved unless he stands up in a meeting, but it is a great help to take a definite step of that sort.*[60]

One suburban meeting hosting 600 participants, despite heavy rain, showcased the stages of commitment for those wanting prayer to receive Christ, which included reflections on the 'after meeting' and personal identification of the need to do so.

> *Test one was the call in the main meeting, test two was to stand for Jesus in the after meeting, and test three to sign decision cards, of which 120 were received... The quiet stillness of God's house became almost painful. Still no response. The tension was hardly bearable. A sigh, a sob, a heartfelt prayer, and then, suddenly, there was a 'sound of a going.' Singly and in twos and threes, in families and whole seats, they arose; youths and maidens of seventeen, old men and women of seventy. An appeal to the chivalry of youth brought twenty-one students to their feet, and another to the young ladies of a neighbouring college was responded to by the same number. And all this was done with the same naturalness and entire absence of anything sensational, that even the most critical could find nothing to carp at. 'All things were done decently and in order.' The church became a valley of weeping, but the tears were tears of joy. The missioner himself was visibly affected, but reminded us that even Jesus wept over Jerusalem.*[61]

Another description of the conversion experience described the process involved.

59. *Southern Cross*, 25th April 1902, 469.
60. *Southern Cross*, 2nd May 1902, 500.
61. *Southern Cross*, 2nd May 1902, 503.

Preparations for Revival

> *A young man who, in response to the missioner's appeal, stands up, and thus publicly declares he is seeking Christ, by that very act does many things. He confesses Christ. He pledges himself, and, so to speak, burns his ships. And a resolve thus proclaimed becomes by that very act much more definite and enduring. Moreover, by thus publicly declaring himself a seeker, the young man attracts to himself the instant notice and sympathy and help of all Christian people. A hundred hands are ready to grasp his; a thousand hearts instantly and almost involuntarily pray for him. He goes into the 'inquiry room,' where he is wisely counselled and tenderly helped; and in the atmosphere of faith and ardor and exultation which fills the 'inquiry room,' he finds the supreme act of faith in Christ easy.*[62]

Use of the after meeting in the inquiry room was explained at one of the suburban meetings.

> *Respecting the methods adopted in dealing with the anxious inquirers, the invitation to voluntarily enter the inquiry room has been found the most effective. Such voluntary action proves conviction and decision. It has been found necessary to exercise great care in speaking to individuals while the meetings have been in progress, indeed only to do so under special circumstances, as some object to attend meetings where such a course is generally adopted.*[63]

These after meetings allowed the consolidation of a convert's decision to follow Christ. Though popularized by Moody, they were used in differing forms by Jonathan Edwards, John Wesley and George Whitefield.[64] Like the evangelist, Charles G. Finney, before him, Moody was concerned with the response of individuals. Whereas Finney used the 'anxious bench' in his services, Moody was reluctant to create a pressured public response, given the uniqueness of the Spirit's supernatural work. The inquiry room allowed individuals to ask questions or seek prayer in what became a more personal work, yet one requiring sufficient assistance by multiple lay people.[65] Throughout his ministry, Moody would seek, where possible, the personal follow-up needed through the assistance of pastors and lay leaders.

Despite the absence of sufficient support in some of the after meetings, the overall commitment of churches to collaborative evangelistic action rode the wave of decades of momentum that had developed since

---

62. *Southern Cross*, 5th June 1902, 76.
63. *Southern Cross*, 2nd May 1902, 505.
64. Bennett, *The Altar Call*, 143.
65. Dorsett, "D. L. Moody," 32.

the United Evangelistic Committee had first appealed to Henry Varley to return to Melbourne. Given, however, the evangelizing passion of the Wesleyan Methodists from the 1830s, it might be said that all of Melbourne's short ecclesial history – especially that of its evangelical churches – had been unfolding to this end. The *Southern Cross* appealed to its readers.

> *For a brief space the churches are to forget their separate interests, and to remember only their common duties. What belongs separately to each is to be laid aside. Denominational boundaries are to grow faint. The energies and resources of the churches taking part in this great movement are to be 'pooled,' and the combined effort, it is hoped, will yield a harvest which will overflow all granaries.*[66]

The united ecumenical investment that was consistently advocated and invested into the Mission's preparation offered a remarkable foundation for the results that were to follow. Many logistical difficulties easily conspire against recommitting to similar efforts today, and yet recapturing the vitalizing energy associated with sustained prayer, organizational cooperation, and ecumenical unity – all essential to revivals before and beyond the 1902 Mission – must surely remain central priorities for all church and denominational leaders. The resultant fruit of revival was certainly in evidence in the four weeks of the 1902 Mission's impact.

Study Questions

1. What do you think of Geil's approach to running 'prayer circles' for a short period, such as seven weeks? Do you think these could operate beneficially today?

2. What is meant by Torrey's motto, 'pray through'? How might we 'pray through' today and what might this look like?

3. What do you think of Torrey's passion to see "thousands of souls converted"? Why does this not seem to happen in some nations to the degree that it used to?

---

66. *Southern Cross*, 7th February 1902, 155.

Preparations for Revival

4. What might have happened if John Virgo had insisted on running the Mission choir, rather than yielding most of the sessions to Charles Alexander? Did this sort of attitude really matter in 1902, and would it matter today?

5. Weekly prayer over many years by ministers from multiple denominations and churches is rare. What do you think allowed it to continue through the efforts of the 'Prayer Band' in the 1890s, even after the death of its founder?

6. Would a gospel presentation in a marquee or a public hall attract people today? To what extent did the intensive effort to pray and door-knock homes play a part in attracting people to Mission events and to local churches?

7. What was the value in conducting 'after meetings' for prayer and counsel? Do you think that this was helpful in receiving completed decision cards? Would the Mission have been a success if decision cards were not collected?

4.
Four Weeks of Revival Impact

Stories from the Simultaneous Sites

As the Mission was launched in Melbourne's various halls and tents, the efforts invested in the months prior began to pay dividends. The four weeks of Mission were described as, "the great evangelizing crusade [that] rattled the dry bones of the Melbourne churches and gathered converts by the thousand."[1] This second revival dimension of widespread evangelistic momentum was in evidence across the month of services in which "nothing of the nature of an entertainment could have drawn such crowds on so many evenings."[2] The *Southern Cross* was delighted to report results from the various sites and was overjoyed by the size of the audiences.

> The biggest hall in many cases proves too little to hold the crowds that come, and the biggest tents not seldom require to have their sides lifted, so that the hundreds who cannot find seats under the tent roof may listen to the singing and hear the preacher. As Mr. Geil graphically put it, "more than an acre and a half of people" had to go away from his service at Footscray on Sunday evening, unable to find room. For once religious services in Melbourne have proved more attractive than the theatres. They have drawn night by night crowds which, in the aggregate, are bigger than those at Flemington on Cup Day!*[3]

1. Virgo, *Fifty Years*, 68.
2. *Southern Cross*, 9th May 1902, 554.
3. *Southern Cross*, 18th April 1902, 423. The Melbourne Cup, still Australia's most prominent annual horse race today, had only recently attracted some 95,000 attendees on 5th November 1901 at Flemington Racecourse. The numbers that would have attended

The Age newspaper reported, too, that the public had "been genuinely interested."[4] A telegram had been despatched to Adelaide requesting the provision of their largest marquee.[5] The crush of crowds and the impact of the speakers became focal in the reports from many centers, such as that from the suburb of Clifton Hill.

> At eight o'clock on Sunday evening black lines of people were filing along the asphalt paths which cross the park land. No tent in Melbourne could have seated them all . . . The [sermon's] language was well chosen, but homely. The style was outspoken and direct. The missioner used no notes. The teaching was explicit. No-one could misunderstand the speaker's meaning. Now and again there was a paragraph of solid reasoning. Between came illustrations drawn from daily life, from literature, from science. Apt Scriptural quotations made good the positions the missioner laid down. The address closed with a persuasive appeal. A more faithful message no man could have uttered.[6]

Geil's presence at Footscray's Federal Hall (which no longer stands) was particularly noteworthy. Some 1,400 assembled in a building with a supposed capacity of 1,200. It was estimated that one hundred conversions were witnessed on the final evening there, inclusive of those of many children, with more conversions again seen each day prior.[7]

> Mr. Geil is a past-master in the art (if you can call it so) of speaking to children. At the close of the service 640 names, including a good many adults, were passed in, as those who had accepted Christ as their Saviour . . . He is tall, muscular, and full of go. His clean-shaven face is very mobile, and his eyes beam with kindness and tenderness, except when some person makes any disturbance when prayer is being offered, or when the Scripture is being read. Then you see the fire flash in the eyes . . . As a speaker, he is fluent and animated, his words being accompanied with considerable gesture. He is fervent at times, and rivets attention, but relaxes the strain

---

Mission events had crowds not been turned away is difficult to estimate and could well have been significantly higher than the average numbers of participants reported.

4. *Age*, 21st April 1902, 6.
5. *Argus*, 16th April 1902, 6.
6. *Southern Cross*, 18th April 1902, 436.
7. *Age*, 25th April 1902, 6.

with some humorous remark. This, however, is done to prepare the way for some pungent application of the truth.[8]

Torrey's much-publicized presence at Hawthorn's Town Hall warranted the use of the nearby St. Columb's school hall as an overflow facility. One service was reviewed as follows.

> *A manly presence, a genial face, a powerful voice, clear and resonant as a bell, are physical gifts which conduce to [Torrey's] acceptability as a speaker. He told his audience that an obstacle which kept him from Christ for six years was his determination to be a lawyer, while he was apprehensive that Christ might want him to be a preacher. Listening to him, one felt convinced that he might have been an eminent barrister, labouring to convince a jury on some question of jurisprudence, or to defend a client. There was no affectation of the learned theologian, although no doubt he has stores of divinity at his command; but he has earnest practical speech, shot through with the light of vivid illustration and flaming with intense conviction. Urging his hearers to take the momentous step on which their spiritual wellbeing hangs, he explained with clearness and reiteration the meaning of the phrase 'accepting Christ.' It meant trusting in the Atonement of Christ for the forgiveness of sin, yielding up to Him the heart and life, to be renewed by His Holy Spirit, and surrendering to Him every aim and purpose that He may rule us every day and to the end of our life. There was scarcely any appeal to the emotions; the speaker preferred to influence the judgment and to arouse the conscience.*[9]

Efforts were made to prioritise the presence of those unaccustomed to church attendance. This continued throughout the Mission, with the *Southern Cross* lamenting at its close that many church attendees had succumbed to the temptation to use the final night's tickets for themselves, despite noting that "great numbers who were unbelievers found admission, and were persuaded to the faith."[10] At a service at Hawthorn, the presiding minister actually urged any Christians already assembled in the host venue to depart, with some leaving to make space for others.[11] In the working class suburb of Footscray, perhaps "the hardest of the vineyards to be tilled,"[12]

---

8. *Southern Cross*, 18th April 1902, 436.
9. *Southern Cross*, 18th April 1902, 436b.
10. *Southern Cross*, 16th May 1902, 581.
11. *Southern Cross*, 25th April 1902, 464.
12. Packer, "Revival No. 1," 278.

failed attempts to secure a 3,000-person marquee led to the need to "restrict, as far as possible, the attendances to persons [who] were not church members."[13] Geil had devised a strategy of his own that led to some 1,300 responding and signing decision cards across the ten nights scheduled."[14]

> Mr. Geil, at Footscray, adopted a plan for giving non-Christians the first chance of seating room. He issued tickets, and announced that Christian people would only be admitted after 7:50; ticket-holders – presumably unconverted ones – having the sole right of admission before that time. The tent at Footscray is crammed every night, and each night finds a number of persons rising in response to the missioner's appeals.[15]

Crowds in Melbourne were reported as ranging from 600 to some 3,000 per night across the suburban centers, with the news media suggesting that the total across the city for the two weeks of services was likely to be 60,000 each evening.[16] This represented an impressive ratio of almost one in eight of the city's 502,120 residents.[17] The estimated half a million attending for the duration of these suburban services alone equalled the entire population of Melbourne (being equivalent to more than five million people attending today).

Stories of individual impact included one that concerned a storekeeper who had facilitated unlicensed gambling and alcohol consumption. After attending a session, he transformed his business to enable Bible studies to take place for the benefit of his many customers.[18] Another drinker and gambler at a particular club was so impacted by one of the tent meetings that he brought nine fellow-members to an Exhibition Building service, after which all were converted, never to return to their clubrooms.[19] A letter was received from one person who fell prostrate on the ground under the "overwhelming power" of the Spirit while reading the Bible at home following a Mission sermon, whereas others began serving as Sunday School workers or expressing interest in overseas mission work.[20]

---

13. Packer, "Revival No. 1," 278.
14. Packer, "Revival No. 1," 278.
15. *Southern Cross*, 25th April 1902, 464.
16. *Argus*, 21st April 1902, 6; Packer, "Revival No. 1," 261.
17. McLean, *Victorian Year Book 1902*, 38.
18. *Spectator*, 6th June 1902, 823.
19. *Spectator*, 4th July 1902, 977.
20. *Southern Cross*, 16th May 1902, 592.

Meetings in Melbourne's Center

After a fortnight of suburban services, a shift to the city center was to be the sole focus for a second two-week period. The Mission's move from local centers to the heart of the city highlighted a Gospel focus for Melbourne long desired by various ecumenical committees and by MacNeil's Prayer Band. The two primary meeting places used were the Melbourne Town Hall (the venue for the lunchtime sessions and afternoon Bible lectures which frequently seated up to 3,000) and the 10,000-seat Exhibition Building which was used for the evening services. While the Town Hall's acoustics made speaking difficult, Torrey claimed the Exhibition Building ensured the second greatest preaching experience of his life.[21] The scheduling did not stop suburban centers wishing to continue in competition, forcing the Mission committee to appeal for a united approach, while recommending "that in all the districts, when the city work is over, aggressive mission work shall be continued by the churches."[22]

Town Hall services were initially advertised to businessmen, so that as attendances exceeded 2,000, women were restricted to the balcony.[23] When women 'had' to be excluded, they demanded a service of their own, so that "businesswomen and factory girls" began to fill the hall from 12:00 to 12:45 pm daily to create "double-barreled" services, with men meeting from 1:00 to 1:45 and with a 3:00 to 4:00 pm Bible reading session being added.[24]

> The attendances at the midday meetings for businessmen and women were as large as ever. Several employers have specially arranged to let their employees attend these meetings. Mr. Geil stated yesterday that the firm of Hoadley had decided to close their factory from 12 to 2 daily, so that their girls might go to the businesswomen's meetings, and the men and boys to the businessmen's services. They were also providing buses to convey the employees to and from the factory.[25]

Punctual finishes saw the women "filing out as a rule between a double line of the men seeking for good places at the next meeting."[26] The business-

---

21. *Southern Cross*, 23rd May 1902, 620.
22. *Age*, 25th April 1902, 6.
23. *Age*, 16th April 1902, 5.
24. *Missionary Review* 1903, 203; Packer, "Revival No. 1," 272.
25. *Age*, 30th April 1902, 6.
26. Berry, "Revival No. 2," 295.

men's meetings were accompanied by the rapid collection of offerings to defray costs, given the extra expenses that had been incurred.[27] The *Southern Cross* was keen to remind its readers that Geil, as a keynote speaker, received no payment other than for travelling expenses.[28]

The 16th April death of Allan Webb, leader of the South Yarra mission and of the Baptist church in the second largest Victorian city of Geelong, was announced by Geil at that day's midday Town Hall service.[29] The *Southern Cross* eulogized: "To call such a death a tragedy would be a denial of Christian faith," and it suggested his death would be coveted because his life had been devoted to the preaching of the Gospel.[30] In addition to Carey's illness and other minor adversities, Webb's death was more significant in highlighting the need for some degree of adaptation to changing circumstances throughout the Mission.

One of the double-session lunchtime events was held on Monday 21st April and saw more than 6,000 frantic people seek entry on what was a public holiday (commemorating the eight-hour working day). Arrangements were hastily made for an overflow service at Melbourne's Independent Congregational Church which was also full.[31]

> *Shortly after 2 o'clock all the doors of the Town Hall were shut; the place was full, and crowds were in the street outside unable to get in. It was amusing to watch how eager groups assailed in turn every entrance to the Hall and all in vain. One weak point in the Town Hall approaches was discovered. It was the little stretch of high iron railing which protects a recess in Swanston Street. This was promptly stormed. A succession of enterprising persons commenced to clamber over it, not a few stout and middle-aged divines, spectacles on nose, performing that surprising feat . . . Now to fill the Town Hall twice in the hours betwixt one and three o'clock with audiences gathered for singing and prayer, while an overflow meeting filled the largest church in the neighbourhood, is a very remarkable feat. It may be safely said that never before in the history of Melbourne, or perhaps the history of Australia, have such multitudes been gathered for purely religious services.*[32]

27. Berry, "The Great Melbourne Revival No. 2," 295.
28. *Southern Cross*, 2nd May 1902, 500.
29. *Southern Cross*, 18th April 1902, 426.
30. *Southern Cross*, 18th April 1902, 423.
31. *Weekly Times*, 26th April 1902, 13.
32. *Southern Cross*, 25th April 1902, 455. Initially, lunch sessions and studies were

It was furthermore noted just how impressive these services were on regular work days.

> To get 3,000 people into the Town Hall, give them a couple of hymns to sing, treat them to a duet by Messrs. Alexander and Virgo, offer up three or four prayers, take up a collection, make announcements, deliver to them an address of 2,500 words, and get them out into the street again , inside three-quarters of an hour, is not a bad performance. And it was done three days last week.[33]

In one of the afternoon Bible studies conducted in the Town Hall, it was observed that people had feared losing their seats if leaving after the previous businessmen's session to eat their lunch. Instead, "they produced frugal meals from bags and pockets and ate them in the hall."[34] With the addition of evening sessions at the Exhibition Building, up to fifteen thousand attended services daily for an unprecedented twelve days in succession.[35]

The first of the combined evening sessions on Sunday 27th April saw many experience difficulty gaining access for the late 8:30 pm commencement, especially those first having attended Sunday evening church services (which accounted for the starting time). This was despite making the entire floor area of the venue available when a curtain sectioning off 4,000 seats was opened.[36] Alexander gently taunted the large crowd as they commenced singing, inducing progressively greater volume and, "with voice, and smile, and gesture, and ready wit, he led them on till every person in the building who could sing – and many who could not – were shouting: 'There's wonder-working power in the precious blood of the Lamb,' at the top of their voices."[37] The crowd sang hymn after hymn, even waving handkerchiefs to one, and were led by a choir of up to 1,250 nightly.[38] Personnel management was no small feat. Choir members were admitted via a badge, and ushers were first required to meet at the nearby Baptist church[39] which also hosted large prayer meetings during the Mission.[40]

held from 1:00 to 3:00 pm.
33. *Southern Cross*, 25th April 1902, 464.
34. *Weekly Times*, 26th April 1902, 13.
35. Berry, "Revival No. 2," 283.
36. *Southern Cross*, 2nd May 1902, 504.
37. *Southern Cross*, 2nd May 1902, 504.
38. Virgo, *Fifty Years*, 68.
39. *Age*, 26th April 1902, 15.
40. *Age*, 30th April 1902, 6.

Four Weeks of Revival Impact

Torrey recorded that, upon his arrival in Melbourne, he had learned that a member of MacNeil's Prayer Band had previously described supernaturally seeing "a vision of great crowds flocking to the Exposition Hall [sic], people hanging on to the loaded street cars wherever they could."[41] This Exhibition Building was typically unable to accommodate the Mission's crowds beyond its maximum 10,000-seat capacity. Many attendees were overheard speaking of the event and singing its popular tunes while riding to work on the city's cable car trams. Torrey became aware that the person who had related the earlier vision had since left Melbourne but traveled a great distance to return and see its fulfilment in person.[42]

At a Y.M.C.A. men's meeting held at the Exhibition Building on Friday 9th May, almost 10,000 filled the seats to hear a sermon from Geil. Handkerchiefs were again waved in a display of patriotic fervor as the national anthem was sung, followed with three cheers for the King, for President Theodore Roosevelt, and also for the Bible. The choir, this time led by J. J. Virgo, consisted of 1,200 male voices. In breaking with the pattern of prior services, a sizeable offering was taken to assist with the construction of a Y.M.C.A. building, with Geil remarking, "I tell you, some giving is better religion than much preaching."[43] After £2,800 was raised, including a single donation of £1,000, Geil preached his sermon, "The Man in the Shadow." It appealed to those present to consecrate their lives in the service of Christ and saw some 7,000 stand in response to the call to salvation.[44] Another special 'missionary meeting' was held on the following Thursday, 15th May, at which twelve organizations were represented as both Torrey and Geil spoke of their own global missionary travels. Every seat was filled half an hour before commencement and thousands were directed to the nearby (Scots) Presbyterian church used as an overflow venue, with many still being turned away.[45]

Despite the constant crush of crowds, not a single accident was reported throughout the Mission, despite police being called on one occasion

---

41. Torrey, *The Power of Prayer*, 48–9. Clara Torrey also used this term in her journal entry description of an evening service, probably recalling a similarly large building of the same name in the Torreys' home city of Chicago (Diary, 23rd June 1902).
42. Torrey, *The Power of Prayer*, 49.
43. *Southern Cross*, 16th May 1902, 582.
44. Geil, *Ocean and Isle*, 300. Mission statistics did not include this number.
45. Geil, *Ocean and Isle*, 301–2.

to regulate the crowds.[46] Hundreds were turned away nightly, sometimes staying for open-air overflow services run by volunteers under the Exhibition Building's main entrance portico.[47] On the last night, too, the rush was "impetuous" as people ran toward the front seats which included those assigned to the leading mission workers on the main platform.[48] Despite the congestion, an enormous choir was retained, and signing was made available for the hearing impaired.[49]

> The main hall at the Exhibition Building was thronged at night, when Dr. Torrey delivered a powerful address on "Heaven, what sort of place it is, and how to get there." At the close nearly a hundred persons rose and entered the inquiry room. The singing, both of the Alexander Chorus of 1,200 voices and Messrs. Virgo and Alexander, is proving an attractive feature of these meetings. A number of new hymns, set to catchy and infectious music, have been introduced, and have already become very popular. Nearly an hour was devoted to music last night. Messrs. Virgo and Alexander sang Pass It On. Dr. Torrey requested the people attending the meetings yesterday to observe today as a period for fasting and special prayer for a blessing on the mission.[50]

Despite a timely close, the after meetings ensured late evenings. Clara Torrey, absent from one of the nightly sessions, noted in her diary: "We sat up till midnight waiting for (host) Mr. Roberts and Archie to come from the meetings. When they came we had cocoa, thin bread and butter, cookies, cake and fruit."[51] Schedules were necessarily compressed, with a typical day's work for Alexander including a central office gathering at 10 am, midday and afternoon services, an evening at the Exhibition Building, and incidental visits and correspondence.[52] Despite this, none of the American guests fell ill throughout the Mission, apart from a brief inconvenience for Torrey caused by a cold and a toothache.[53]

46. *Southern Cross*, 23rd May 1902, 620.
47. *Age*, 5th May 1902, 5.
48. *Argus*, 10th May 1902, 15.
49. *Age*, 28th April 1902, 6.
50. *Age*, 30th April 1902, 6.
51. Clara Torrey, Diary, 23rd June 1902.
52. Williamson, *A Great Revival*, 28.
53. *Leader*, 10th May 1902, 26.

Four Weeks of Revival Impact

Initial Impressions

Journalist, J. A. Packer of the *Daily Telegraph* observed that "a cyclone could not have struck Melbourne more effectively than did the great Simultaneous Mission."[54] Witnesses were effusive in their praise of the event and its impact upon individuals, churches, and the city. While not quantifying the perceived result, their statements captured the mood of the various denominations who had invested significantly into the Mission. The following were published in the *Southern Cross*.

> *The immediate effect on the whole community has been for good – good without question. The religious life of the town has been wonderfully stimulated. (Rev. John Carrington – Anglican).*

> *The mission has had the general effect of awakening interest in religion in the community to an unusual degree. People have been talking about the things of God everywhere. There is a perceptible willingness to be spoken to about personal religion . . . There is a general quickening to the pulse of spiritual life. (Rev. A. Davidson – Presbyterian).*

> *The general effect of the Mission has been to lift the various churches out of a self-centered individual life into a healthy recognition of their larger duties and broader relations. To this fact the marvelous sweep of the Mission is due . . . Church membership has been translated from a complacent sense of possession into a keen perception of debt. This carries with it the guarantee of a working church; and a working church means the evangelization of the world. (Rev. S. J. Hoban – Methodist).*

> *Everywhere the voice of praise is heard. Families have been greatly blessed. The whole aspect of some homes is changed. (Rev. W. Williams – Methodist).*[55]

Aside from personal transformation such as from alcoholics who lost their desire to drink,[56] widespread spiritual regeneration was in evidence. The report of the E.S.A. was published as follows.

---

54. Packer, "Revival No. 1," 258.
55. *Southern Cross*, 20th June 1902, 763.
56. Packer, "Revival No. 1," 263.

> *Your committee rejoices in being able to report that the year which has just concluded has been the most successful one in the history of the Society. It began in a time of general depression: all the churches had the same experience; conversions were few, worldly conformity among church members was increasingly manifest, and the features which marked the Church in Laodicea were only too plainly the features of the Church in Victoria. Faithful men in different parts of the state were deeply impressed with the need for revival of spiritual life, and unknown to each other they made it a subject of earnest prayer. These prayers were answered, and today we give thanks to God for multitudes who have been led to listen and to embrace the Gospel of His grace.*[57]

In writing for an English audience, William Warren reflected on the Mission's success.

> *Whole families were brought to Christ, as well as infidels, publicans, and actresses. The 'Decision Day' among the children was a day of ingathering, and, among others, the boys and girls in the colleges were reached. In one Sunday School every scholar in the first three classes of young men and women openly confessed Christ. One Christian Endeavor Society has received an addition of fifty members as the result of the mission. A suburban church has had two hundred new members added, while in one suburban Sunday School, on 'Decision Day,' more than one hundred scholars openly gave themselves to Jesus Christ, each professing convert right through the mission signing an acceptance card.*[58]

Reuben Torrey Jr. later claimed that his father's campaigns were more successful than those of others because of his logic, his avoidance of emotionalism, his insistence on joining a church, and his commitment to encouraging the studying of the Bible.[59] Numerous stories existed of converts entering ministry, with one woman reporting to Alexander that seven boys, inclusive of her brother, had done so in the one church.[60]

---

57. *Southern Cross*, 10th October 1902, 1156.
58. *Missionary Review* 1903, 202.
59. Martin, *Apostle of Certainty*, 192.
60. Davis, *Twice Around the World*, 351.

Aftermath

After four weeks in Melbourne, a series of Mission events was organized that took Torrey, Alexander and Geil to different locations around Australia and New Zealand. Geil subsequently continued with his global missionary tour. Virgo initially accompanied Geil to Brisbane and was invited to accompany him internationally but declined due to his extensive Y.M.C.A. responsibilities.[61]

Geil's subsequent explorations included a less overt focus on preaching than in Melbourne, but with no diminished enthusiasm for missional fruitfulness. Geil sought primarily to endorse and enhance local missionary efforts as the best-placed forms of leadership for local impact. The scope of his journeys and the intent to showcase the conditions of missionaries to his American readership demonstrated with conviction his own extensive support of global mission work. Geil's visit to British East Africa (now Kenya), for example, included affirmation of the important work he saw unfolding.

> *The testimony I am able to give as an eyewitness is that missionary work in this lofty district is a monumental success and worthy of liberal support.*[62]

Torrey and Alexander, however, continued their ministry Australia-wide in the months beyond Melbourne, but then returned to the city where they were farewelled at two concurrent Valedictory services held on Monday 6th October 1902, one at the Melbourne Town Hall and the other at the nearby Independent Church. Torrey addressed ministers on the priority of Bible reading and prayer. It was said that "there was not a recess that could possibly hold another occupant.[63] The Reverend C. H. Nash moved that the meeting, "representing the Protestant community of Victoria, and also many who had received blessing and help in the Simultaneous Mission," should express its deep obligation to Torrey's church in Chicago for releasing him to preach the Gospel in Australia.[64]

Torrey's first and subsequent address in London, "What the Simultaneous Mission in Melbourne Proved," summarized the circumstances by which Torrey was invited to Australia. Having believed that prayer was central to the Mission's success, he now advised his London hearers that the

---

61. Virgo, *Fifty Years*, 69–70.
62. Geil, *A Yankee*, 55.
63. *Argus*, 7th October 1902, 6.
64. *Southern Cross*, 10th October 1902, 1157.

5,000 people in prayer for his desired global revival were now praying God's blessing on the services in England.[65] "The dawn has brought delight in Australia," Torrey announced. "Soon the light will burst upon this favored land," he concluded.[66] He was clear in his belief that a revival had been catalyzed, one also now being supported indirectly by the undergirding efforts of the prior prayer intensives of Chicago and Melbourne.

The confidence taken into mission fields beyond Melbourne was undoubtedly associated with the growing momentum created by a significant initial harvest. Far from merely generating short-term religious fervor, the reaping of 8,642 professed converts in just four weeks was a result comparable with the greatest of those witnessed in the most fruitful campaigns of D. L. Moody, whose own presence in Melbourne had earlier been sought.

Before considering the impact of the third element of revival, the effect of the transforming message of the missioners, it is important to understand these evangelists themselves. Their individual contribution, background, and style, are investigated in the next chapter, as is the contribution of Torrey's relationship with the trustees of the Moody Bible Institute to his decision to come to Melbourne.

Study Questions

1. To what extent do you think that the Christian heritage of the people of Melbourne may have affected the attendances and conversions seen in 1902? How does this balance with other factors that may have been involved?

2. What would need to happen today for the kind of impact that reaches as many people collectively as the number actually living in the city? Could evangelistic services play a part? What would be the role of the internet?

3. Do you think that people define sin in the way that they once did? How does this matter when it comes to helping people understand the Gospel? What is the essence of Christian salvation and how could your definition help to win people to Christ?

---

65. *Southern Cross*, 27th February 1903, 210.
66. *Southern Cross*, 27th February 1903, 211.

4. What do you think contributed most to the willingness of people to attend daily lunchtime and evening evangelistic sessions in such large numbers, over and above attendance at weekly church services?

5. Is there something uniquely impacting about a large choir leading a congregation to sing, or are different contemporary musical forms equally inspiring?

6. What is your impression of the results of the mission? Although follow up by churches remains important, why is it difficult for churches to secure new commitments to faith?

7. What do you think of Reuben Torrey Junior's later impressions about his father's success? Are the factors he raised important today?

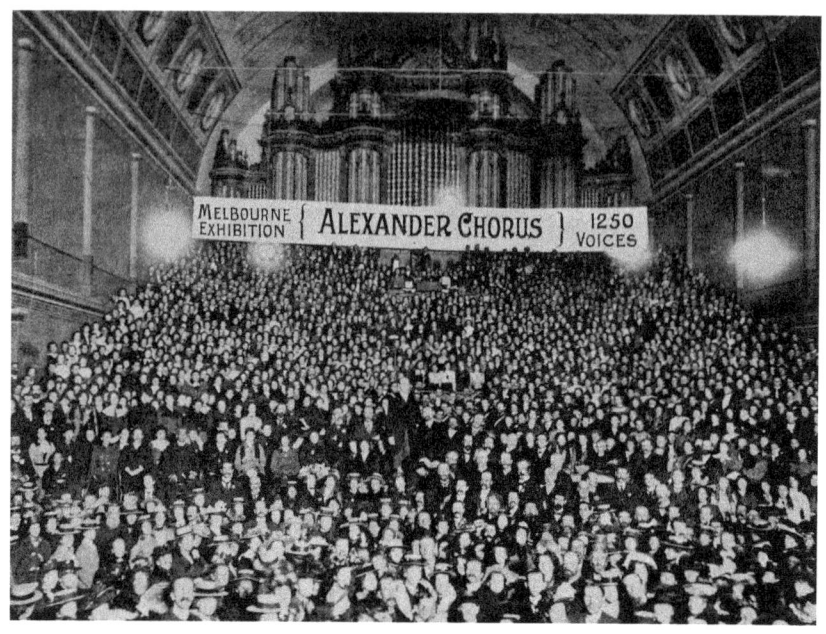

Alexander's Choir at an Exhibition Building service

Alexander's Choir beneath the advertisement of the Y.M.C.A. servwice with W. E. Geil

R. A. Torrey

W. E. Geil

Charles M. Alexander

S. Pearce Carey (Mission Chairperson)

Exhibition Building, 1902

Exhibition Building, 2024

Melbourne Town Hall, 1902

Melbourne Town Hall, 2024

The 'Glory Song' (from the first edition of *Alexander's Revival Songs*, 1902)

Interior of a suburban meeting held at the Federal Hall, Footscray

Interior of the Exhibition Building

Robert Harkness, mission pianist and Torrey biographer

Evangelization Society of Victoria with James Balfour, President (upper right), Charles Carter, Secretary (bottom right), and G. P. Barber (front row, second from left)

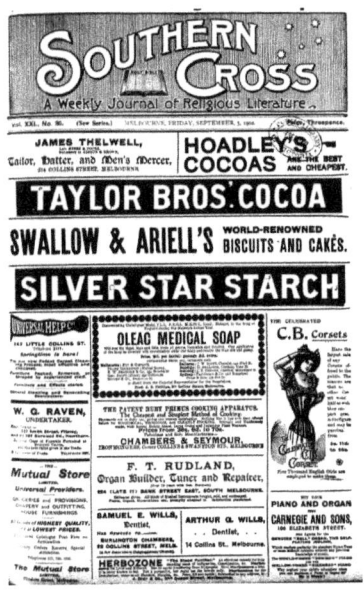
Southern Cross (1902 masthead)

Southern Cross (special edition)

West Melbourne tent mission with Robert Robertson

5.

Leadership of Revival

A Role for Three Americans

The combination of Missioners, with their contrasting personalities, played no small part in the success of the Melbourne event. Extensive prayer, unprecedented unity, and the ablest of coordinating efforts were complemented by the choice of Geil and Alexander to aid the work of Torrey who had been intended as the 'headline act.' Geil only met Torrey for the first time when they discovered that they were on board the same ship from Hong Kong in "a blest conspiracy of circumstance."[1] Whereas the various Sydney sites had featured Geil with local ministers, they reached barely beyond 20,000 people. While he had helped to secure the 3,000 or more conversions there, Geil had less influence than in Melbourne. Despite complimenting Sydney's commendable organizational efforts, though, he believed more could have been done, concluding for instance that the greater involvement of "laymen" in support of the follow-up of converts would have aided the work of the clergy.[2] Beyond the Melbourne event, Torrey and Alexander visited Sydney but, with smaller choirs and fewer conversions, the most significant results were said to be in the strengthening of the churches,[3] with the most prominent services there perhaps being the midday services for men.[4]

---

1. Carey, "Conspiracy of Circumstances," 256.
2. Geil, *Ocean and Isle*, 180–1.
3. Williamson, *A Great Revival*, 62, 64.
4. Martin, *Apostle of Certainty*, 151.

The Simultaneous Mission services were not universally well received, however. Despite largely positive press responses nationally, the *Sunday Times* in Western Australia included a brief review of both the Sydney and Melbourne events. Headed, "The Guile of Geil," it also appeared to assume Torrey's early presence in Sydney, despite his brief visit there occurring *after* first appearing in Melbourne.

> Geil and Torrey, the two Yankees, struck their rich evangelizing field in Australia by accident. They happened along in Sydney while the churches here were conducting a simultaneous mission. They became somewhat insignificant helpers, but their cheap-jack ways of making spiritual salvation a land of bargain-counter novelty gave them a vogue among the young women and anaemic youths of whom their audiences were chiefly composed. Being a class who when they see a good thing 'push it along,' they swooped down on Victoria when the game was through in Sydney and took spiritual charge of Melbourne, with the aid of a clever press agent whom they took, after the manner of enterprising circus proprietors, from Sydney. The manner in which these two Yanks have been able to move the religious world of Victoria by their claptrap phrases and indecent familiarity with sacred themes has disgusted all earnest Christians.[5]

Such criticism was sparse, however, and the plaudits kept coming. *The Age* found Geil to be "impressive" and Torrey "forcible."[6] *The Argus* described one of the Melbourne events as "enthusiastic," being led by an "inspiring" Alexander.[7] Despite no Catholic participation, even the *Catholic Press* conceded that the various services were successful and mostly "sound in Christian doctrine."[8] Melbourne's satirical *Punch* was surprisingly complimentary and commended the style that was effective in enabling the conversion of a diverse range of hearers.

> It is possible that the methods they employ are just as necessary to stir those quiet souls as to bring the more effeminate and frivolous to a tearful repentance. We take no exceptions to the methods of Mr. Geil and his friends, Mr. Alexander and the Rev. Dr. Torrey.[9]

---

5. *Sunday Times (Perth)*, 29th June 1902, 4.
6. *Age*, 3rd May 1902, 10.
7. *Argus*, 12th April 1902, 19.
8. *Catholic Press*, 30th August 1902, 17.
9. *Punch*, 1st May 1902, 1.

While the Mission was often referred to as a story of the success of Torrey and Alexander[10] who were nevertheless integral participants, the addition of Geil's complementary persona reinforced the Mission's overall impact, with the *Leader* observing that Geil "keeps his large audience greatly interested, and at times highly amused."[11] The leadership of each of the key personnel was to contribute a vital ingredient to the impact of the Mission for its duration. The general style of the American keynote speakers was assessed as follows, noting the appropriateness and importance of humor and of pressing for the decisions of their converts.

> *They are not afraid of moving their audience to laughter. They light up truth with wit and deliberately translate it into terms of humor. Is all this, some hearers ask, quite in harmony with the reverent temper of a religious service? We frankly think it is. We think there is a real place for humor in religious teaching. Every experienced speaker knows that there is a philosophical justification for the use of humor as a means of persuasion. Some people, again, object to the methods employed for bringing people to a decision. They are asked to stand up, or to lift the hand, as a sign that they are willing to begin Christian life. And to some people, this represents an effort of almost historic courage . . . No one imagines that the act is itself essential to salvation; but it represents something that is essential. For most people, the mood about religion is one of nebulous indecision, of uncertain and changing emotions, of vague desires that never crystallize into purpose. Excitement is a mischief when it hurries us into some path where we must turn our back on both conscience and reason.*[12]

William Edgar Geil

William Edgar Geil (1865–1925) of Doylestown, Pennsylvania, was little known in Melbourne before 1902 but quickly grew in the estimation of many, prompting journalist, J. A. Packer, to recognize his potential to be

---

10. This link was evidenced in the titles of publications such as Davis's biography, *Torrey and Alexander: The Story of a World-Wide Revival*, Maclean's biography, *Torrey and Alexander: The Story of their Lives*, and Williamson's monograph, *A Great Revival*, whose subtext referenced "The Story of R. A. Torrey and Chas. Alexander."

11. *Leader*, 19th April 1902, 26.

12. *Southern Cross*, 25th April 1902, 463.

"the greatest evangelist of the first quarter of the [twentieth] century."[13] Geil had embarked on his "Great World Wide Tour," a missionary expedition that had begun with visits to Hawaii, Fiji, Tonga, New Guinea, the Philippines, and New Zealand.[14] On commencement, he had been placed in a cabin with an Australian businessman who had previously funded S. Pearce Carey's investigation of American ministry methods. Though initially seeking in vain to have that cabin to himself, Geil quickly formed a friendship with his fellow occupant that helped to introduce him to Carey who brokered invitations to Australia. When meeting with Carey in Melbourne, he became aware of the E.S.A.'s invitation to Torrey. Agreeing to use Geil's own experience in partnering with Torrey, though, enabled Carey to strengthen the Mission coordination efforts.

Packer, in his account of the Mission, referred to Geil extensively. Describing him as an energetic and humorous speaker, Packer rated him second only to Moody in ability, and the Mission's "commanding figure and dominating influence, a splendid example of sanctified audacity."[15] *The Age* newspaper marveled at Geil's "kaleidoscopic" capacity to adapt to different audiences.[16] Prominent Anglican clergyman, Canon Digby Berry, determined that, if Geil "were not a consecrated man, he would shine as an actor," noting that humor was rarely absent from his sermons which also demonstrated a pathos that "reached the conscience."[17] Melbourne's *Weekly Times* further elaborated on Geil's ebullient persona.

> William Edgar Geil is a speaker of great force and capacity for attracting and holding the attention of his hearers, and has a fund of humorous illustrations. He adopts unconventional methods in his addresses, makes his point at one moment with a story or a quip that will rouse a smile, or maybe a laugh, and at another with an earnest pathos that awakens a responsive chord in his audience. With a practiced skill he can play upon the emotions of his audience in a way that enables him to impress more clearly the teachings he wishes to instil into their minds.[18]

---

13. Packer, "Revival No. 1," 268.

14. Geil's subsequent travels extended to China, Burma, Korea, Kenya, and the Congo.

15. Packer, "Revival, No. 1," 267–70.

16. *Age*, 16th April 1902, 5.

17. Berry, "Revival, No. 2," 284.

18. *Weekly Times*, 19th April 1902, 13.

The *Southern Cross* added: "There are few men who can hold an audience with such perfect command. With Mr. Geil there are no lulls; everything goes off to the tick, and the twenty-five-minute sermon seems like five."[19] An assessment was also made of Geil's involvement in a midday Town Hall service, his speaking craft somewhat resembling modern oratory.

> *Mr. Geil came forward to give out the announcements. He stands over six feet, and wears a long grey frock-coat, which makes him look taller than he is. His face is clean-shaven, and intellectually strong, though not markedly handsome, and his voice, which must have once possessed the sweetness and fulness of a trumpet, has been worn down by continued open-air speaking till it has got something of the huskiness of the foghorn – though, to be sure, it has a good deal of the force and carrying power of that same useful instrument. Mr. Geil is a journalist as well as an evangelist. He appreciates a striking incident, or a racy story, at its full value, and in his addresses he uses the taking headlines, so to speak, and the catchy paragraphs that are the peculiar features of American journalism . . . Promptly at 1:20 he begins his address – after taking a preliminary throat tonic consisting of egg and cayenne. Anything further from an ordered sermon would be hard to imagine. It is not an address of the 'firstly – secondly – thirdly – moreover – and lastly' kind but rather a succession of vivid word pictures, a single line of thought and many side issues – 'more side-tracks than trunk line' an American might label it.*[20]

Berry further observed that, in keeping with the practice of the early apostles who framed the Gospel using points of cultural identification, Geil would find common ground with his hearers from which to articulate understanding.[21] Sympathetic to his manner and methodology, Berry identified an originality and impact that prompted spiritual birth. This was not merely the commencement of life but a crisis event occurring after it had already begun.[22] Questioning by what alternate methods Geil's detractors might draw crowds of up to 10,000 people, Berry placed the responsibility for the lasting results of the mission on fellow ministers who would help to consolidate new faith commitments by "prayer and the ministry of the Word."[23]

19. *Southern Cross*, 9th May 1902, 539.
20. *Southern Cross*, 18th April 1902, 435.
21. Berry, "Revival No. 2," 286.
22. Berry, "Revival No. 2," 288.
23. Berry, "Revival No. 2," 288, 295.

Leadership of Revival

Geil was said to be capable of endless variation in his "vivacious, entertaining" style.[24] Virgo noted Geil's "informality" and the "alternation of dry humor and earnest emotion."[25] Clearly, some had objected to his preaching style, prompting a light-hearted response.

> *I hear that some good folk are objecting to my style of preaching the Gospel. Well, I've been thinking I would advertise a meeting, and gather together all those people who think it an awful crime for a man to be jolly and talk religion with a smile on his face. I would hold the meeting in an undertaker's shop. We would have four undertakers there, and forty gallons of embalming fluid; and I guess we'd fix 'em.*[26]

It was also claimed that the Mission showcased "too much of the successful Philadelphia lawyer, too many flashlight photographs, and too little kneeling."[27] Geil again defended himself against his critics, clearly taking exception to their insistence.

> *Daresay they're good Christian people but they're the kind who would have caught hold of David's coat tail and said, "See here, don't you go out without Saul's armor on." They wouldn't believe in the smooth stones from the brook, though those stones had the power of God behind them. Tell you what, if you who write me these letters would spend the same time on your knees back of a dry-goods box, with some soul longing to find Christ, you would be good for something. Yes, I get mightily tired of that sort of thing. If anybody doesn't like my style, let them go and preach better.*[28]

To the charge that Geil was an irreverent jester, the *Southern Cross* retorted that it had "seldom met a soul of such consuming zeal," concluding that "he that is near him is near the fire."[29] Unaccustomed to humorous preaching, the Melbourne audiences revelled in Geil's manner. In one service, he adopted a boxing stance. "See that? That's free will," Geil remarked. "If you don't believe it, get in front of it, and that will be predestination."[30] When

---

24. *Herald*, 16th April 1902, 4.
25. Virgo, *Fifty Years*, 68.
26. *Southern Cross*, 25th April 1902, 465.
27. *Age*, 29th May 1902, 4.
28. *Southern Cross*, 25th April 1902, 483.
29. *Southern Cross*, 16th May 1902, 581.
30. *Age*, 18th April 1902, 6.

facilitating a collection in a Town Hall business meeting, he quipped, "Pass the plate quickly, but not so fast that you can't put your money in."[31]

Virgo was convinced of the lasting impact of such a style, having met many people in the years following the Mission who had made "lasting changes for the better." Conceding that some may have come "simply to amuse themselves," they remained to understand the messages being preached. Virgo commented poignantly: "If, then, it needed unconventionality of teaching to shake the deadly complacency of these folk, surely no more [needed to] be said to justify unconventionality."[32]

Reuben Archer Torrey

R. A. Torrey (1856–1928), too, was not averse to the use of quick-witted humor, as observed in his response to the claim that, in the absence of modern amplification, he could not easily be heard. To his request for the hands to be raised of those who could, and then could not, hear him, Torrey responded with resulting laughter: "Just look at them, poor things. They didn't hear what I said."[33]

Torrey had come to the attention of Warren and Barber on the strength of his preaching and its apparent suitability for the interests of the spiritual leaders of Melbourne. *The Age* newspaper referenced Torrey's "exceptional gifts as a platform speaker," noting that his voice was "melodious and flexible, with a good range," and that he tended to speak with "fluency and characteristic American directness."[34] At the commencement of the Mission, Melbourne's *Weekly Times* sought to familiarise its readers with this visitor with whom they were as yet unacquainted.

> *The Rev. R. A. Torrey is a native of New Jersey, and is 46 years of age. After graduating at Yale College he was ordained at the Congregational ministry in 1878 and took up his first pastorate. He met Mr. Moody, the evangelist, in the same year. After a period of study in Germany he became superintendent of the Minneapolis City Missionary Society in 1886, became superintendent of the Moody Bible Institute in 1889, and obtained the pastorage of the Chicago Avenue Church in 1894. This church was built and equipped by Mr. Moody,*

---

31. *Age*, 18th April 1902, 6.
32. Virgo, *Fifty Years*, 68.
33. *Southern Cross*, 18th April 1902, 436c.
34. *Age*, 14th April 1902, 5.

and will hold 2,500 people. Mr. Torrey is at present superintendent of the Bible Institute in Chicago, and he has been head of the International Christian Workers' Association for seven years. He takes the lead at all of the large gatherings which are held throughout America by the Christian Workers. Some of these gatherings are attended by 20,000 people, drawn from all classes of the community. Dr. Torrey is now on twelve months' missionary tour of the world. He has visited China and Japan, and it is interesting to note that the Buddhist priests of Japan, the most conservative class in the world, provided several converts to the teachings of the preacher. Ceylon, India and Great Britain are yet to be visited. Physically, Dr. Torrey is an imposing man. He weighs 15½ st., can preach six times in a day, and so powerful is the carrying capacity of his voice that he has preached to upwards of 15,000 people with success. The Moody Bible Institute, with which Dr. Torrey has been for years prominently connected, is a great institution. Over 400 students, male and female, attend there and are trained for all classes of Christian administrative and mission work, home and abroad, and for Sunday School work. They are also trained in Gospel music. Dr. Torrey is still head of this institute, but is taking a year's vacation in the form of a year's hard work and travel. As a writer, he is, perhaps, best known as the author of "How to Pray," "How to Win Men to Christ," and "What the Bible Teaches."[35]

Said to be a theologian and teacher, rather than an evangelist or preacher,[36] Torrey's message was described as "a flaming sword; God has made him as a polished shaft – in his quiver he has kept him close."[37] The *Spectator* noted that he had "a way of impressing upon the hearer's mind, not the speaker, but the Master whom he serves."[38] His manner was described by biographer, J. Kennedy Maclean.

> *Dr Torrey, it is true, is not an emotional man. He cannot weep with men, as other great preachers have done, as he pleads with them to come to Christ, for he is not built on that plan, and his appeal is more to the intelligence, the common-sense, and the conscience than to the heart. But yet there is a wonderful softness in his nature. Listen to him as he faces a crowd of drunken men and women and tells them of the love of Jesus. No word of reproach falls from his lips.*

---

35. *Weekly Times*, 19th April 1902, 13.
36. *Herald*, 16th April 1902, 4.
37. *Argus*, 7th October 1902, 6.
38. *Spectator*, 25th April 1902, 589.

> *In simple language he speaks of the Saviour's love in such a manner that the hardest conscience is awakened and the coldest heart touched.*[39]

Despite what was to become a stunningly successful international tour over a two-year period, a less noble facet of Torrey's Chicago ministry became a significant contributing factor to his travels. The Moody Bible Institute's apprehension over Torrey's views on faith healing had centered on a desperate plea made to the unorthodox and controversial healing evangelist, John Alexander Dowie. Dowie would later establish the ten square mile 'Zion City' in Chicago, and then preach in Australia, claiming to be Elijah the prophet. He had earlier held several Australian pastorates, including in Melbourne where he had narrowly escaped death in a dynamite attack on his church premises when departing the building earlier than expected. Dowie was already aware then that he had "public enemies," and the city's *Herald* newspaper imagined that, "however little a person may sympathise with Mr Dowie in other respects, he [would] get the hearty sympathy of the public in connection with this affair."[40]

Torrey had now sought out Dowie to pray for his daughter suffering with diphtheria just a month after he had also lost another daughter to the same condition. Opportunistically, Dowie included Torrey's correspondence of 14th April 1898 two years later in his *Leaves of Healing* newspaper when escalating tensions with Moody began to be directed to Torrey several months after the former's death. Torrey's appeal had contained a frank admission.

> *DEAR DR. DOWIE: - Four weeks ago today we lost a daughter aged nine years and twelve days by diphtheria. For twelve or more years none of our children had taken medicine, and they had all been healed in God's way, this one included.*
>
> *The morning Elizabeth passed away, very early. Mrs. Torrey came and told me she was choking. My faith failed and, ultimately, I went for a physician. I asked guidance before going, but now believe after asking guidance I went my own way, not God's; the way of unbelief, not the way of faith. The passage about Asa's seeking to the physician and not to the Lord came to me as I went, but I put it aside. The child died.*

---

39. Maclean, *Torrey and Alexander*, 63.
40. *Herald*, 3rd September 1885, 3.

> Today our daughter Blanche has the patches, parched throat, and that indicates diphtheria. I have anointed her, and believe God has heard. She is already decidedly better, the patches partly gone and backache all gone; but Mrs. Torrey especially wants you and Mrs. Dowie to come over and pray, and to examine us to see if you can find any sin in the way.
>
> We see nothing to hinder an immediate cure. I know it is a good deal to ask so busy a man to come; and, if you cannot, any way remember us in prayer.
>
> You may, if you like, read this letter publicly. I believe I have dishonored the Lord and would be glad to have people know the failure was not in Him, but in me. Sincerely yours, R. A. TORREY, 39 Pearson Street.
>
> Pearson is one block north of Chicago Avenue, and our house is five doors east of North State.

Appended to Torrey's letter, was a further note.

> Friday Morning, 9:20. I took this to the Tabernacle and afterward to the Home yesterday, and did not find you in. I think, however, I had better send it. Blanche is decidedly better. Had a good deal of pain during the night, but it is gone. The patches are almost entirely gone from her throat and the sore and hard cord back of the ear is now soft as anyone's, but she is not entirely well yet. Please pray for her. I think God does a perfect work.
>
> Sincerely yours, R. A. TORREY.[41]

Of concern to the Institute was not merely the association with Dowie himself, but also the rejection of medical assistance on the basis of faith. Torrey had belatedly sought help in a perceived moment of weakness, and now astonishingly assessed that his trust in God had been lacking. Despite the appended follow-up to the original correspondence verifying that Dowie could not have been responsible for his daughter's improved condition, the revelation in March 1900 of Torrey's 1898 actions and healing beliefs was unsettling. Dowie's receipt of an earlier letter from a member of Moody's church seemed to have provoked an increased animosity towards Moody

---

41. *Leaves of Healing*, 10th March 1900, 642-3.

and Torrey when it apparently alleged Moody had called Dowie a "crank." Dowie's April 1899 response to that letter was swift.

> Mr. Moody, you had better deal with that Torrey crank who is the Superintendent of the Moody Bible Institute. He says he believes in God as the Healer of His people. What are you going to do about it? If I am a crank, what is R. A. Torrey? Come, Mr. Moody, let us have this thing out.[42]

In reply, Moody had communicated his apparent risk mitigation strategy via his son, Will Moody, in a response which placed Torrey at odds with his Chicago colleagues.

> In the Bible institute I absolutely refuse to allow the teaching of Divine Healing to be presented, and should a student refuse medical assistance in case of sickness, he would either have to leave the Institution (thus relieving us of all responsibility in the case), or send for some competent physician to attend him.[43]

When Moody died in December of 1899, Dowie did not hesitate to lay the blame for his passing upon Moody's failure to adhere to the practice of faith healing: "He paid the penalty of his rejection, and of his setting aside God's Word." For Torrey's willingness to stay with the Institute and Church, he was deemed to have cursed both, leading Dowie to add: "May God in His infinite mercy speedily remove him."[44] This prayer, perhaps answered in part only by means of Torrey's departure for subsequent international travels, reveals the depth of feeling concerning a doctrine which proved decisive enough to find little expression in Torrey's future ministry.

Indeed, sensitivity to the Dowie controversy may have undergirded a strong response from Torrey at an address given in Melbourne on 27th April 1902 when an interjector called out, "What about Dowie?"

> I am going to talk about realities, not frauds. If there is anyone come here tonight for the purpose of making silly interjections and interrupting the work of God, he had better leave right now, because we cannot lose 6,000 people for the sake of one crazy man. Anyone who interrupts, or makes a disturbance, will be at once handed over to

---

42. *Leaves of Healing*, 8th April 1899, 461.
43. *Leaves of Healing*, 24th March 1900, 699.
44. *Leaves of Healing*, 24th March 1900, 699.

> *the police, and will be prosecuted. All those who agree with me, and are in favor of this procedure, hold up your hands.*⁴⁵

To the sight of hands raised throughout the congregation, Torrey curtly followed up: "Carried unanimously," before continuing with the service. Torrey had earlier reflected upon Dowie's legacy.

> *A great many of his elders left him when he proclaimed himself Elijah. His own father, too, has left him. The secret of his success is that he terrifies people by making them believe that if they leave him he has power to kill them. Then he claims to heal, and, as people value health more than anything else, that attracts attention to him. He is undoubtedly a 'fake of the first water.'*⁴⁶

As to Torrey's own legacy, his pianist and biographer, Robert Harkness, gave a positive affirmation of his character as a prominent minister.

> *His conscience was never seared by the blight of sinful folly in the pursuit of doubtful notoriety. His mind was never obscured by the cloud of pretense in any form. His heart was never divided in its devotion to God. He elevated evangelism in every detail of his work.*⁴⁷

Charles McCallon Alexander

Charles Alexander (1867–1920) held early memories of singing Gospel hymns used by Moody and Sankey when seated with his family by the fire side. Alexander's mother would also read Moody's sermons to him. Then, in 1884, a sixteen-year-old Alexander was present when both Sankey and Moody visited Staub's Theatre in Knoxville. He was so impacted by the autobiography of evangelist, Charles Finney, too, that he read it a second and third time. When his father died, he became convicted that safety with God mattered more than anything else and promised to commit to serving him when receiving an assurance of salvation. Alexander claimed that "a great longing to save souls came" to him that night and remained thereafter.⁴⁸

This led to a short exhortation during his later song leading in Melbourne. He asked on one occasion: "I should like to know how many of you here have family prayers in their homes?" When the response was less than

---

45. *Southern Cross*, 2ⁿᵈ May 1902, 500.
46. *The Leader*, 12ᵗʰ April 1902, 25.
47. Harkness, *The Man*, 127.
48. Alexander, *A Romance*, 30.

adequate, he pressed for an identification of those who would begin a new habit until extracting the greatest possible show of hands.[49]

Torrey noticed once they had worked together that Alexander studied other song leaders until he could improve on them. Alexander indicated that he would tire of his work "if it were not for the soul-saving part of it."[50] When in Australia, Alexander addressed his approach to this interest: "Some will say that they have tried hard to get souls for Christ and have no results to show; that's not your business, you do what you can to win them and leave the rest to God."[51]

The *Weekly Times* reported on Alexander's credentials.

> *He is a man of striking personality, who has done great work as an evangelist in America. He had three years [of] training at the Institute superintended by Dr. Torrey. One American paper, referring to his mission work, writes:— By the magnetism of his presence, and the beauty of his singing, he calls up from their hidden depths all that is best and tenderest and sweetest in the human heart, and the great audience sways to his hand like a ripe wheat field in the breeze. It melts to tears under his pathos of song, and ripples to laughter at his good-humored wits. Mr. Alexander, writes the Southern Cross, has had a stirring career in the States as a leader of singing at evangelical conventions. He is young, strong, vigorous, has an excellent baritone voice, and a genius for conducting. Early in life he consecrated his musical gifts to the service of the Lord, and has co-operated with some of the greatest evangelists in America— notably the late Dwight L. Moody, W. B. Williams, and Dr. Torrey. He went through the great World's Fair gospel campaign with Mr. Moody: a similar campaign at the Atlanta Cotton Exposition [sic] in 1895, and has appeared before great audiences of from 2,000 to 10,000 almost daily for the past three years.*[52]

At a later stopover in Melbourne in 1907 for a 'song service,' Alexander returned to the Exhibition Building, witnessing another sea of faces and leading an enormous choir of 1,500. He received hearty applause for his sentimental remark, "Good old Melbourne."[53] By 7:30pm, half an hour before the scheduled commencement, the doors were closed on hundreds.

49. Alexander, *A Romance*, 53–4.
50. Alexander, *A Romance*, 13.
51. Alexander, *A Romance*, 14.
52. *Weekly Times*, 19th April 1902, 13.
53. *Age*, 5th April 1907, 6.

Ten thousand people gathered inside for an evening program supported by J. J. Virgo and Robert Harkness.[54] At the preliminary choir practices, people were also turned away by the hundreds.[55]

Alexander's next return visit with J. Wilbur Chapman in 1909 was also significant, and later termed "a time of Pentecost for the whole Commonwealth,"[56] given the large attendances. The impact was less pronounced during a subsequent visit by the pair in 1912 where both were briefly indisposed due to illness.[57] Clearly, the 1902 Mission had served as an important template and inspiration for these future events. In 1909, Chapman observed that many of those who had been converts in 1902 were now serving in ministry.[58] Also, a Unitarian (or 'nontrinitarian') minister who had challenged Torrey in 1902 before being convicted of fraud was later converted under Chapman's ministry, claiming as the reason "the unanswerable conviction of Dr. Torrey's statement regarding the deity of Christ."[59] It was, perhaps, only with the onset and devastation of the First World War that the appetite for such Simultaneous Missions largely abated. Alexander would not return to Australia after 1912.

Samuel Pearce Carey

S. Pearce Carey (1862-1953) was a great grandson of the famous missionary to India, William Carey. He had been a minister in England when called to the prominent Collins Street Baptist Church in central Melbourne in 1900 by a wealthy sponsor who insisted that he first seek insight into American ministry models. He later became president of the Baptist Union of Victoria in 1903 before returning to England in 1909.

Upon meeting him, Carey served as the interface between Geil and local leaders who forwarded their letters of introduction. Carey believed that it was entirely appropriate that this capacity to introduce Geil to Australian contexts be his responsibility, having "recently seen and studied the work of so many leaders in America."[60]

54. Alexander, *A Romance*, 127.
55. Davis, *Twice Around the World*, 351.
56. Alexander, *A Romance*, 153.
57. *Age*, 4th May 1912, 17.
58. *Age*, 10th August 1909, 4.
59. Harkness, *The Man*, 39.
60. Carey, "Conspiracy of Circumstances," 244.

As chair of the Mission, Carey attended a September 1901 meeting of the Victorian Council of Churches which was inspired by stories of England's Simultaneous Mission of 1901 from Rev. J. G. Greenhough, the visiting President of Britain's National Council of Evangelical Free Churches. At the meeting's close, it was resolved to attempt the arrangement of such a mission in the Autumn of 1902.[61] Carey had undoubtedly heard accounts of the Sydney mission held in November from his deputy, Rev. S. C. Kent, who spoke at public gatherings there.[62]

Illness at the time of the Mission's opening did not prevent Carey from taking the stage for its most prominent moments. Keeping his "ear to the telephone," he took great delight at reports of "considerable inroads" having been made with those outside the Church, believing "work begun with deep conviction of sin" to be unlikely "to pass away."[63] Later, on the occasion of his own farewell service in 1909, Carey reminded his audience of the foundation of Christ, saying, "I would have no hope for my own development or for the future of mankind except in Christ, but because I believe in that Son of God I have unlimited hope for all men."[64]

John James Virgo

Jack Virgo (1865–1956) was general secretary of the Young Men's Christian Association and one of the four secretaries of the Mission. An athletic and impassioned leader, he was an enthusiastic cricketer (being a friend of English great, W. G. Grace) and was seemingly the first person to bring the sport of basketball to Australia in 1894 before the Y.M.C.A. played in the first organized game which was held in Adelaide.[65]

Virgo had become secretary of the Y.M.C.A. in Adelaide in 1887 and also began Sunday evening evangelical services which attracted more than a thousand people in which he conducted the choir, sang, and preached. In 1900 he became secretary of the Australasian Union of Y.M.C.A.s. Virgo was later appointed secretary of the Y.M.C.A. in Sydney in 1903 and general secretary of the London Central Y.M.C.A. in 1911.

---

61. Carey, "Conspiracy of Circumstances," 243.
62. *Sydney Morning Herald*, 2nd December 1901, 5.
63. *Southern Cross*, 5th June 1902, 84.
64. *Watchman*, 7th January 1909, 1.
65. Virgo, *Fifty Years*, 34.

Virgo's support of Geil during the Melbourne Mission was noteworthy, continuing in other locations in the weeks following. He was also noted for his preaching on occasions throughout the event, with one resulting in a crowd that grew "till there were more outside than in, and results were not wanting."[66] The *Southern Cross* affirmed Virgo's impact.

> Mr. Virgo is a fine singer, and he sang solos frequently at the services addressed by Mr. Geil, as well as preaching when required. He sang at one of the Exhibition meetings the well-known solo, "Where is my wandering boy tonight?" with wonderful expression; and it was so much appreciated that he was asked to repeat it at the midday meeting on the following day. While the air was still vibrating with the chorus which follows the second verse, a young man sprang up in the audience and cried: "Here he is, and he is coming back to Jesus today!" The young fellow proved to be a drunkard and an atheist, who had been touched by the words of Mr. Virgo's solo.[67]

Despite his diverse talent and his role with the Y.M.C.A., Virgo's humility in yielding to Alexander as the choral leader of the Mission typified the collaborative ecumenical spirit in evidence at the time. The leadership of the mission, however, required a distinctive message, one articulated by the characteristic voices and personalities that maintained noteworthy unity within their evident diversity. It is to the nature of this message that we now turn.

Study Questions

1. What was the importance of having several international guests leading the Mission? How do you think they may have complemented each other? Could the Mission have been negatively affected if Geil had his way in securing a single-berth cabin aboard the ship to Melbourne?

2. What do you think of the criticisms levelled at the speakers? Does their approach to dealing with it offer suggestions as to how we might prevent criticism from undermining churches and ministries today?

---

66. *Southern Cross*, 18th April 1902, 436c.
67. Williamson, *A Great Revival*, 28.

3. Geil was said to use an "alternation of dry humor and earnest emotion." How does the balance of humor and emotion help communication? How important are these elements?

4. Are there aspects of the reporting and eyewitness testimony that you find jarring? If so, how could these be addressed as productively as possible?

5. What is your assessment of Torrey's interactions with John Alexander Dowie? Would you act differently in similar circumstances?

6. Why might Dowie have attributed Moody's death to a lack of support for his healing ministry? What is the possible motivation for people's similarly blunt comments about such ministry today, and how should we react to them?

7. What do you notice about the manner of Charles Alexander that made him successful? What shapes musical excellence in churches today and what limitations exist in this area?

6.

The Transforming Revival Message

Structuring Mission Services

The third revival element – the impacting and systematic revival message delivered by known missioners – brought intentional transformation. Prior to the commencement of Melbourne's Mission, the *Southern Cross* declared that it was to be welcomed in bringing "an agreed and public witness to the fact that the end for which all churches exist is the conversion of men."[1] English missioner, F. B. Meyer, highlighted the importance of evangelistic preaching required in any Simultaneous Mission event.

> *If I may be forgiven the presumption, I would say that the less the address is like a sermon the better. People hear sermons enough and, on the whole, the missioner is not expected to deliver a discourse, with its heads and subdivisions, but to make an appeal for decision, based on the Word of God, baptized in the power of the Spirit, and lighted up with suitable incidents and illustrations, which will convince the judgment, touch the emotions, arouse the conscience. In most cases people have already been taught the way of salvation, and are ready to admit the duty of repentance and faith, but need to be led to take the final step across the line.*[2]

The preaching was nevertheless inspirational and favorably evaluated in the Melbourne press.

> *That evangelists like Dr. Torrey and the sprightly Mr. Geil do work crowds into a condition approaching hysterical is true . . . This effect*

1. *Southern Cross*, 7th February 1902, 155.
2. *Southern Cross*, 21st March 1902, 318.

> *of their methods is obvious; it is a plain fact, too, that the religious enthusiasm provoked does not remain with the bulk of the converts, but when the froth has passed off and the waters are still, there remains a large amount of actual good in thousands of quiet, steadfast hearts.*[3]

With a style clearly unfamiliar to those accustomed to the more measured preaching adopted in Sunday services, Torrey and Geil nevertheless engaged their audiences quickly. In one of the few church buildings used as a suburban mission venue, the *Southern Cross* bemoaned the positioning of the pulpit, being too far from the packed crowd, given the typical evangelist's desire to be "in close proximity to those he addresses." The requirement for sufficient space was also important due to the preference for enforcing appeals and ensuring connection of "the action to the word," such was the demonstrative flair of the body language adopted.[4]

The approximate format of the mission sessions may be gleaned from an examination of one particular service conducted in this same church venue. Opening at 8:00 pm with an organ recital, the choir members took to the stage with the key missioner, Stewart Byron, and five attending ministers. After the singing, a prayer was offered, and hymns were then sung either side of the reading of a passage relevant to the sermon for the evening. The preaching, on this occasion delivered by one of the other ministers present, followed intercession made in response to some specific requests for prayer. It closed with an impassioned plea.

> *"Come with the vain struggle to save yourselves, and lay the fruitless effort down. Come with all the sorrows and troubles of life, and lay them down before Him. Who can comfort and relieve? Come with the burden of sin, and He will cast all your sins into the depths of the sea."*[5]

It was reported that the 'after meeting' continued without interruption before the final benediction. The majority of the congregation of some 600 to 700 remained to then hear Byron address the solution to the problem of sin, closing with an appeal that they might trust in God so that life eternal would be assured.[6] Those responding were then invited to the vestry at the

---

3. *Punch*, 1st May 1902, 1.
4. *Southern Cross*, 18th April 1902, 440.
5. *Southern Cross*, 18th April 1902, 443.
6. *Southern Cross*, 18th April 1902, 443.

conclusion of the service, so that they might hear further on the matter. An evangelistic impetus was clearly felt throughout the Mission at events such as this one, being held day after day and with speakers imploring those in attendance to surrender to Christ.

Themes of the Mission

The Missionary Review of the World listed several ingredients of success in the Melbourne Mission, as articulated by Torrey, these being: (a) the power of believing and united prayer; (b) the power of the inspired Word of God; (c) the power of the atoning blood of Christ; and (d) the power of the Holy Spirit.[7] These factors were affirmed in his first London address after the Melbourne Mission as Torrey prepared to replicate his Australian impact.[8] He believed that the message of future revivals had now been scripted, suggesting that the same fourfold emphasis would ensure similar outcomes in England as those seen in Melbourne.[9] Further distilling this insight to identify just one main overarching reason for the Mission's significant results, though, Torrey was clear that it was not the preaching or the singing, as such, but the undergirding importance of prayer.[10]

Sermons preached in Melbourne both by Torrey and by Geil (see Appendix 2) made particular reference to conversion, as well as to turning from the corrupting influence of sin. This was dependent, in turn, on the divine power outworked by the activity of the Holy Spirit. Torrey's methodical and structured delivery of biblical sermons revealed a prominent use of apologetic faith defences, equipping his audiences in the mold of the Institute educator he had become in Chicago. Geil was the more expressive and energetic speaker, less doctrinal but equally focused on evangelistic impact and social commentary.

Torrey, in particular, believed Baptism with the Holy Spirit was a definite and knowable experience essential for any Christian's successful impact.[11] Its connection with personal holiness and Christian service therefore saw it strongly linked to evangelistic success.[12] Torrey illustrated

---

7. *Missionary Review* 1903, 220.
8. *Southern Cross*, 27th February 1903, 210.
9. *Missionary Review* 1903, 804.
10. Williamson, *A Great Revival*, 80.
11. Torrey, *The Baptism*, 10.
12. Torrey, *The Baptism*, 14.

these notions in key Mission sermons, while also citing his own experience of the Spirit in 1894 under the leadership of Moody who had declared, "I can see no reason why we should not pray today just as definitely as on the Day of Pentecost, that the Holy Spirit should come upon us."[13] Typical Torrey statements on the role of the Holy Spirit were reported by the *Southern Cross*.

> *The baptism of the Holy Ghost will refine a man in five minutes. It is a slow process getting rid of our sins in any other way, but a baptism of fire does it at once.*[14]

> *Many men are trying to walk in the strength of a baptism they received twenty or thirty years ago. It won't work! I have been baptized with the Holy Spirit, thank God; but I want to be filled again this afternoon.*[15]

As Torrey would pray that the Spirit's power might come upon his hearers, he invited those willing to surrender to stand to their feet. Hundreds rose on one occasion while Torrey prayed earnestly that God would pour out the power of his Holy Spirit.[16] Though a forerunner (and thereafter a contemporary) of Pentecostalism, Torrey was opposed to any notion of evidential tongues, yet he shared the view that encounters with the Spirit subsequent to salvation were needed for optimized service.

By comparison with the later and better-known preaching of Billy Graham, several observations can be made. Like Torrey and Geil, Graham was strongly focused on the need to be freed from sin through Christ and to enjoy a conversion experience. All three speakers highlighted the importance of themes such as prayer, the Church, money, right belief, Heaven and Hell, and even preaching itself. Torrey and Geil, however, showed a slightly greater focus on the work of the Spirit and the existence of social evils (reflective of broader evangelistic influences at the time). They were noticeably less nuanced than Graham in addressing their hearers as sinners in need of God, referring regularly to the presence of agnostics and atheists in their services, even happily branding those who had not sought Christian salvation as "infidels." Graham's 1959 sermons delivered in Melbourne were more inclined to reference faith, prayer, and the power of God to change

13. *Southern Cross*, 25th April 1902, 477.
14. *Southern Cross*, 16th May 1902, 586.
15. *Southern Cross*, 25th April 1902, 476.
16. *Southern Cross*, 25th April 1902, 477.

lives. While evangelistic delivery and content might understandably reflect personal styles and a degree of adaptation to cultural mores, the prominent preachers of two different revival eras in the same city maintained unmistakable clarity in articulating the problem of sin and the need for salvation through Christ alone.

Contentious Views

Moral objections to various social practices were evident throughout the 1902 Mission, noting strong Temperance influences in Melbourne at the time which polarized views on the selling and consumption of alcohol. Torrey stridently castigated any seller of liquor as "either a murderer or a murderer's accomplice," despite preferring to focus his evangelistic efforts on "respectable sinners" who he believed to be the worst transgressors of all.[17] Geil's objection to the sale and use of alcohol was similarly clear.

> *A man gets cursed with drink, his wife is cursed, his children are cursed, and when he goes the length of his tether he is hid away in the cell of a prison. I am against it, I tell you. Let the drunkard have his liberty, and lock up the man who made him drunk.*[18]

For Torrey, anything not done for the glory of God was problematic, and new converts were encouraged to speak to at least one person daily about the state of his or her soul. Women were advised to spend less on gloves and more on the salvation of the "heathen" and, in response to a question on the legitimacy of singing secular songs in public, Torrey advocated the use of Gospel songs instead, that God would perhaps work through them "for the conversion of some precious soul."[19] Explicit objections were raised against smoking, ballroom dancing, and even the theater.[20] Asked, too, about the merits of card playing as a means of keeping young people at home, Torrey feared a progression to gambling. "The euchre party is the kindergarten of the gambling hell," he stated.[21] Geil cited concern over causing others to sin, in accordance with 1 Corinthians 8:13. When asked about dancing

---

17. *Southern Cross*, 16th May 1902, 580.
18. *Southern Cross*, 9th May 1902, 539.
19. *Southern Cross*, 9th May 1902, 530.
20. *Argus*, 24th May 1902, 14.
21. *Southern Cross*, 9th May 1902, 538.

he simply stated, "I don't dance, because it isn't right for me to."[22] Torrey concurred, noting that "there is not a modest woman who would let any man except her husband put his arms around her in a waltz,"[23] and also that "liberties are permitted between man and woman that are not permitted elsewhere in decent society."[24] Melbourne's weekly *Punch* magazine objected.

> *The Rev. Dr. Torrey disapproves of dancing and declares it to be productive of all sorts of iniquities. "If the girl knew what a man thinks when he is dancing with her she would never dance again." Here arises the question: "How do you know, Dr. Torrey? How are you in a position to say what a man thinks?" As a matter of fact, the reverend evangelist knows no more about the thoughts of the male dancer than his (the dancer's) partner does, probably not nearly half as much, because it is usual for a man when waltzing to converse with the lady dancing with him. A few men may have confessed to Dr. Torrey that they think this or that when dancing, but that does not substantiate his claim by any means. In fact, a man in the position of the evangelist speaking against dancing must make wholesale charges to produce an effect, but when looked into the charges are not worth a button. The man who thinks evil when dancing thinks evil when walking or talking, or sitting, because he is built that way, and Mr. Torrey is in the position of the man who blames the mill wheel for making the water run. All sorts of men go dancing, and all sorts of women, but all sorts do not necessarily think nastiness, and dancing is not in itself nasty. Let us try and teach men and women to meet with clean, honest minds, and there will be no need to abuse dancing, which is like abusing smoke as the cause of fire.*[25]

The Age newspaper reported Geil's conviction that even Sunday travel should be prohibited in the interests of rest, a conviction which later saw him remain in Melbourne on a Sunday, rather than spend it traveling to Sydney.[26]

> *At the businessmen's meeting Mr. Geil announced the receipt of a letter taking him to task for apparent inconsistency in denouncing Sunday travelling, while a notice had been issued under the name of*

---

22. *Southern Cross*, 9th May 1902, 538.
23. *Age*, 29th April 1902, 6.
24. *Argus*, 19th June 1902, 5.
25. *Punch*, 12th June 1902, 2.
26. *Southern Cross*, 1st August 1902, 916.

The Transforming Revival Message

> the mission giving a schedule of Sunday trains suitable for persons desiring to attend the Exhibition meetings. Mr. Geil explained that the card had not been issued by his consent or with his knowledge. Neither he nor Dr. Torrey was concerned in advertising Sunday trains. He wished the notice had never been issued. He had no sympathy with the Sunday train business. He had fought the question in America, and would continue to do so. The poor man and the working man had just as much right to the Sunday as the rich man.[27]

The *Southern Cross* was prompted to issue an explanation concerning the cards.

> It afterwards transpired that the cards were privately issued by one of the suburban choir conductors for the purpose of letting members of his choir know what trains they could catch in order to reach the Exhibition in time to join the choir there.[28]

Conversion

In reflecting on the initial impact of his preaching at afternoon gatherings, Torrey published the following in his Chicago journal, the *Institute Tie*, noting the number of older men amidst his converts, these apparently being less likely than others to embrace the need to redirect their lives.

> When I had finished I told them that I did not wish any one to stand but those who had not been Christians before, and who had now fully settled it that they would accept Jesus Christ as their Saviour, and surrender to Him as their Master, and begin from today to confess Him openly before the world, and strive to live to please Him in all things, and to be out-and-out Christians. I went over it and over it to make it plain. Then I gave them opportunity to rise. They began by ones, twos, fives. Charles Alexander thought that there were about eighty of them, strong men. The number of grey-haired men among them was remarkable.[29]

Publicly responding to preaching had been a practice prominent in past missions in Melbourne, but Torrey did not limit its use to conversion. In speaking on the power of the Holy Spirit, Torrey emphasized responsiveness to a dimension of Christian empowerment less prominent in churches

---

27. *Age*, 29th April 1902, 6.
28. *Southern Cross*, 2nd May 1902, 504.
29. *Institute Tie* 1902, 367.

at the time. A suburban meeting at Hawthorn showcased the impact of such follow up to Torrey's preaching in this regard.

> *Last week, when Dr. Torrey pressed home the necessity of the new birth under the Spirit's operation, and called upon those who are professing Christians, and who felt that they were not partakers of the Holy Spirit's work, to stand up, quite a considerable number arose. It was a pathetic sight in one aspect, and in another it was an occasion for rejoicing. It was sad to think that so many had gone on, up to that hour, content with a form of Godliness, and it was at the same time a joyful thing that they should be willing to acknowledge their spiritual destitution, and to press into the realization of the blessings of the Kingdom . . . Those who had previously risen were invited to come forward, and in a few moments the meeting assumed the appearance of an old-fashioned Methodist revival. Ministers of various churches in the vicinity, and other workers, male and female, were talking, Bible in hand, to the seekers, or praying with them, and, amid the singing of hymns, and the low-toned conversations with those who were passing through the crisis of their lives, there was such a wave of religious feeling as few in the building, perhaps, had ever known.*[30]

In preaching for personal transformation, however, Torrey was routinely clear about the expectations of converts who would respond to their need for Christ.

> *They had to keep away from sin altogether. It was not sufficient to feel that an act was not wrong; they should feel absolutely sure it was right before acting. They should do nothing unless they felt it would please God, and act just as they felt Jesus Christ would act were He in their place. "Do you think that Jesus Christ would play cards at your place?" demanded Dr. Torrey. "Don't do anything you would not be willing to do when the Lord comes. Would you like the Lord to find you with a cigar in your mouth, or at a theater, or in a ballroom?" Converts were warned against doing anything that was not for the glory of God. They should surrender themselves absolutely to Jesus Christ, and make others converts.*[31]

The *Spectator* observed that Torrey "appeals first of all to the mind, but his words find their way to the heart; he sets people thinking and the

---

30. *Southern Cross*, 25th April 1902, 467.
31. *Argus*, 24th May 1902, 14.

thoughts abide."[32] Torrey would conclude his Exhibition Building sermons with an "appeal to sinners," after which people typically "rose in all parts of the building," so that half of those in attendance remained for the after meeting.[33]

Geil similarly pressed for public responses to his sermons, with a challenge given at the 'great missionary meeting' service (on 15th May 1902) for all "to stand up who were willing to go out as evangelists of the heathen if God should open the way for them to do so," after which 200 responded. Geil then reverted to his more usual urge for personal salvation.

> I then asked all who were willing to accept Christ as their own personal Savior then and there to publicly declare Him as their Lord, to arise and stand . . . scores arose. The great audience then stood en masse, and for five minutes sang while people passed to the inquiry room.[34]

Geil insisted upon coordination of services, in contrast to the approach of some who would prefer relative inaction while "trusting the Holy Ghost."[35] At his suburban meetings, the rows of seating would include two 'workers' assigned to six attendees. The workers would possess an identifying badge, a booklet containing suggestions for interaction, and printed slips for completion by those accepting Christ. Three minutes were allocated for workers to speak with those near them before the ending of the first part of the service. Geil asked for those who had been Christians for over ten years to stand, then five, and then two. As he worked down to include those newly responded, others would join, and the names of a hundred or so would be collated without noise or sensationalism.[36]

Geil advocated evangelistic endeavor and taught a method by which his hearers could be equipped to engage in personal conversion. When speaking to some 1,500 people about this at the public holiday gathering held at the Independent Church, an overflow service from that held at the larger Melbourne Town Hall, Geil offered his 'Spots' method of evangelism (see Appendix 3). Presenting thousands of envelopes with black, red and yellow discs of adhesive gummed paper, these were affixed to certain pages of the Bibles brought by those present, protruding from the edges where

32. *Spectator*, 25th April 1902, 589.
33. *Southern Cross*, 2nd May 1902, 504.
34. Berry, "Revival No. 2," 304.
35. *Southern Cross*, 18th April 1902, 436.
36. *Southern Cross*, 18th April 1902, 436.

they marked key passages. The black spots referenced verses focused on the problem of sin. Geil encouraged the reading of these texts with those who were not yet Christians, confident that they would be convicted of their need of God, and declaring that "the Word of God is a chariot of the Spirit of God."[37] The red spots were to mark the verses the Christian could read with people to lead them to faith if convinced of their own sin.[38] The yellow spots represented prayer to assist Christian living.[39]

Geil's systematic reference to passages of Scripture to lead people to faith required a greater openness to Bible reading than that typically seen today in a secular society in which fewer than half of all adults identify as Christian.[40] After all, could a methodology that allows the biblical text to compel conversion by engaging with its content really suffice today? It is not particularly dissimilar to a successful contemporary approach to Bible reading advocated by David and Paul Watson leading to the baptism of almost one million new Christians and the planting of thousands of new churches globally.[41] Their use of Bible reading 'Discovery Groups' prefers guided reading with individuals to traditional Bible studies in the interests of contextualising, but also de-culturalising, the Bible so that the text might speak to the world of the hearer without the interference of external presumption.[42] Was Geil's approach any less constructive to this end?

The Music of the Mission

T. Shaw Fitchett, son of the *Southern Cross* publisher, W. H. Fitchett, recalls a meeting with Charles Alexander, held at the ornate temperance hotel in Melbourne, the Federal Coffee Palace. The meeting was significant for the publication of what was to become 'Alexander's *Revival Songs*,' the hymn book of the Mission. Fitchett recalled the 1902 encounter.

> *I remember well, how he drew what he called a 'cut' from his pocket and asked if we could print a few thousand leaflets from it. It was a block of the 'Glory Song.' In half-an-hour we were more than half-way to loving each other; in another ten minutes we were off*

---

37. Geil, *Ocean and Isle*, 305–6.
38. Geil, *Ocean and Isle*, 307.
39. Geil, *Ocean and Isle*, 308.
40. McCrindle, *The Changing Faith Landscape*, 12.
41. Watson and Watson, *Disciple Making*, xiv.
42. Watson and Watson, *Disciple Making*, 17, 128–9.

> *to the Coffee Palace for dinner and a yarn. Before I left that night, I had made him disgorge all the 'cuts' from his trunk, and all the hymn-prints of which he had the rights, and persuaded him to let me rush up a complete hymn-book. Within a week or ten days, his first hymn-book was on the market, supplying him with the means to set ten thousand people singing.*[43]

It was said that Alexander was able to teach the multitudes to sing "familiar songs which had, in time past, been rendered with no particular feeling."[44] The "Glory Song" made its international debut in Melbourne despite being better associated with the later Welsh Revival.[45] It was published in the *Southern Cross*[46] and was said to have "set Australia on fire."[47] Alexander recalled, however, that his first encounter with the song, written by popular hymn-writer, Charles H. Gabriel, was far from positive. Believing Gabriel had "wasted a page," Alexander dismissed its potential, only to reconsider when later hearing it sung. Recalling that he could think of "nothing else for days thereafter," it then "captured Melbourne in a single night."[48]

> *At the close of our first revival campaign in Melbourne it seemed to me that everybody in the city was singing the 'Glory Song.' People going away on the suburban trains were singing it. Brass bands played it, and it was sung and played in all sorts of out-of-the-way places.*[49]

The song appeared in print some 17,000,000 times within just five years and was translated into seventeen languages.[50] Alexander later said, when discussing its success, "I look at a Gospel song as a sermon – a sermon on wheels, and when you teach a good Gospel song to a man, it is like starting a wagon down a hill with the brakes off."[51]

Torrey was adamant that music played a key evangelistic role in the Mission: "It is often the instrument used by God for the salvation of sinners. Many a sinner has been converted while listening to the singing of the

---

43. Alexander, *A Romance*, 52.
44. Williamson, *A Great Revival*, 18.
45. Davis, *Twice Around the World*, 106.
46. *Southern Cross*, 18th April 1902, 436d.
47. Davis, *Twice Around the World*, 139.
48. Alexander, *A Romance*, 65.
49. Alexander, *A Romance*, 65–6.
50. Davis, *Twice Around the World*, 19.
51. Davis, *Twice Around the World*, 352.

hymns."[52] Torrey claimed that the Melbourne experience included the best singing he had ever heard in any services in which he had been involved.[53] Its prominence was enhanced by the expertise of the musical leadership provided by the likes of Virgo and Alexander, the latter's vigorous efforts to engage the throng finding their characteristic and optimum expression with the emphatic singing of the opening line of the refrain of the Mission's signature song: "Oh, that will be glory for me."

> *A few silver notes float up from the grand pianos. They are faint, but unmistakable – they are the preliminary bars of the 'Glory' song, and there is a thrill of recognition. 'When all my labours and trials are o'er,' sing the choir; 'And I am safe on that beautiful shore,' adds the right gallery; 'Just to be near the dear Lord I adore,' chimes in the left gallery; 'Will through the ages be glory for me,' shout the people on the floor. Then the man on the island – who has been responsible for these bursts of song – goes off into violent Indian club exercises, and a word, 'Everybody!" comes floating up, to be chased by such a volume of melody that the roof rings to the shout, 'Oh that will be – Glory for me.'*[54]

One minister observed, after watching Alexander at work, that he should "put as much life into [his] preaching."[55] The foreword to Alexander's *Revival Songs* – the precursor to Alexander's later hymn books (known by various names) – assessed the impact of the opening Town Hall service. "Mr. Alexander is, of course, a conductor of the first order," it noted, while observing in the enthusiasm of ministers attending the Mission services that "nobody had suspected the parsons of such singing gifts."[56] Alexander's magnetism in coordinating the music of the Mission was aided by the use of his choir of in excess of a thousand voices. The singing was accompanied by an organ, two grand pianos and a brass band.[57] Male voices represented just one tenth of the choristers, so that Alexander's harmonies were not fully heard,[58] although the sheer number of volunteers involved

---

52. *Southern Cross*, 16th May 1902, 580.
53. *Southern Cross*, 23rd May 1902, 621.
54. *Southern Cross*, 9th May 1902, 539.
55. *Southern Cross*, 16th May 1902, 582.
56. No author, *Alexander's Revival Songs*, foreword.
57. *Age*, 6th May 1902, 4, and 24th May 1902, 8.
58. *Punch*, 17th April 1902, 9. The 1909 Chapman and Alexander meetings consisted of a choir deemed by *Punch* to be "more artistic, better harmonized, than that of 1902 which was far more womany" (20th May 1909, 2).

was impressive. Alexander later stated that he had "never dreamt that a choir could sing with such fervor, snap, and go as they had done," stating it was the largest choir he had ever conducted.[59]

The pianist accompanying Alexander throughout the Australian and New Zealand events, Robert Harkness, was son of the mayor of Bendigo, a large regional gold town. Despite his initial absence of a personal faith, Harkness had offered to play for Alexander's visit. He was disinterested in the hymns but was nevertheless quickly able to memorize them. Harkness improvised accompaniments which were approved, despite actually hoping that they would "displease" Alexander. Rather than either evangelist reacting to his playing as he had hoped, Torrey simply asked Harkness if he was a Christian.[60] Alexander requested that Harkness board a train later that day for a series of services in another Victorian township. Harkness committed to following Christ that same afternoon.[61] He continued his support of Alexander in India and the U.S.A.,[62] working with him for twelve years.[63]

At the great converts meeting of 23rd May, 8,000 tickets were sent to registered Mission converts, with these being checked upon entry.[64] An expanded choir of 1,800 was formed.[65] Most of the 6,000 converts in attendance had already joined local churches and "almost all those who had not united with the church as yet, promised to do so at once."[66] Alexander offered some advice at the conclusion of the evening. His use of a 'year text' offered a single verse on which to base the shaping of one's life over the coming year. Alexander suggested 2 Timothy 2;15, "Study to shew thyself approved unto God." He proceeded to tell of its prior use in replacing usual greetings between colleagues. The text reference had once been shouted by Alexander from a departing train to one such friend who was waiting on the adjacent platform. When a bystander was startled at hearing the reference, he proceeded to look it up and made a personal profession of faith.

---

59. *Argus*, 24th June 1902, 5.
60. Davis, *Twice Around the World*, 48.
61. Davis, *Twice Around the World*, 49.
62. *Argus*, 7th October 1902, 6.
63. Alexander and Maclean, *A Romance*, 199.
64. *Southern Cross*, 10th September 1902, 28.
65. *Age*, 24th May 1902, 8.
66. Torrey, *The Power of Prayer*, 49.

Alexander had the Melbourne converts shout "Two-Timothy-two-fifteen" back at him three times before bidding his farewell.[67]

As the mission drew to a close, and decision cards were forwarded to churches for the all-important post-event follow-up, the mission organizers undoubtedly began to wonder what the prevailing impact was likely to be. Was there some possibility of significant social transformation in the city? Could the churches expect to see significant growth? Was the revitalization in evidence across the four weeks likely to continue to be felt in subsequent Sunday worship services? Few could possibly have imagined that the reverberations of one Australian city's mission would continue to be felt far afield as its influence began to reach into multiple nations in the years ahead. It is in considering this fourth of revival's key dimensions within the Melbourne Mission that we examine not only the prolonged impact on the church and society in the city but also, in this case, that which was felt well beyond it.

Study Questions

1. Are the preaching themes used in this Mission still valid today? Glance at the sermons reproduced in Appendix 2. What do you notice about their content or emphasis?

2. What is your impression of the format of the suburban mission conducted by Stewart Byron? What is an effective service format today and why is this important?

3. Are there any differences between the themes of the Mission's preaching and that of Billy Graham many years later? What preaching differences do we use intentionally today? How are these helpful or necessary?

4. Are there any problems with the stance taken on alcohol consumption, dancing, gambling, and Sunday travel? What position should be adopted today on similar matters?

5. What do you think of Torrey's advice for converts? What would you retain from it in contemporary church services or conversations?

---

67. *Southern Cross*, 30th May 1902, 656.

6. Are there helpful elements of Geil's 'Spots' technique for securing conversions and aiding discipleship (see Appendix 3 for further information)? What are its strengths and weaknesses?

7. What does a "sermon on wheels" look like today? Are there songs that communicate truth helpfully? Are there some songs that you have grown to like, but did not like initially (just as Alexander grew to love the 'Glory Song')?

7.

From Local to Global Revival

Assessing Conversions

Recorded responses provided an initial measure of the impact of the Simultaneous Mission, although there was some degree of difficulty in quantifying the long-term sustainability of faith commitments made. Alexander Stewart, the South Richmond missioner and a future Presbyterian moderator, admitted that numerical results were merely a "rough gauge of the work" best proved through "subsequent steadfastness."[1] Further prayer and effort from Christians would be needed to ensure that those won to faith could persevere. The *Southern Cross* suggested that "the committee responsible for the Mission [would] be wise to let figures severely alone" on the basis that results could not "be condensed into arithmetical symbols."[2] Instead, the fourth of the dimensions of revival under examination here is its overall impact on churches and on the broader community and, as we shall soon see, on the global Church.

At the conclusion of the 1902 Mission, Torrey was interviewed by the *Southern Cross*. Whilst affirming the need for conversions at such evangelistic events, he indicated a desire for "a great arousing of the churches," so that the revival would continue well after the evangelists had departed."[3] For the evangelists and organizers, the month-long campaign was about much more than mere headline results. The Methodist *Spectator* captured a telling sentiment in this regard.

1. *Southern Cross*, 5th June 1902, 69.
2. *Southern Cross*, 16th May 1902, 579.
3. *Southern Cross*, 5th June 1902, 87.

> *But the leaders of the Mission never counted as actual converts those who stood up or raised their hands. On the contrary, when we asked Mr. Virgo at the end of the first mission week for the numbers then recorded, he said, "You can get the figures at the office if you like, but we would rather not publish them. We don't look upon them as satisfactory tests. We believe that many who raise their hands are not converted, and that many who don't raise them are." Furthermore, in this Mission, no one can say that Drs. Torrey and Geil, and the other missioners too, have not insisted on the need of true repentance as the necessary precursor of saving faith. That doctrine was faithfully proclaimed, and strenuously insisted upon. It is quite true, as our esteemed friend says, that something more than the mere fact of the Town Hall being crowded at noonday and the Exhibition Building at night is required as proof of the reality of the work. But no one could look at the "sea of earnest faces," fixed and motionless, upturned towards the speaker without feeling that an Unseen Power was stirring their hearts.[4]*

Noting this caution in claiming statistical success, the number of self-identified converts was nevertheless remarkable in comparison with other similar missions. Across Australia and New Zealand, the 1902 Mission produced some 20,000 declared converts in almost five months.[5] The 8,642 recorded in Melbourne's four weeks of services[6] compared very favorably with the national total, and also with the figure of almost 3,000 seen in Torrey's similar four-week visit to Edinburgh the following year.[7] In two-and-a-half years of services in Great Britain, interspersed with visits to mainland Europe, in excess of seventy thousand decisions were registered throughout England, Ireland, Scotland and Wales, with results in most cities surpassing those obtained by Moody,[8] although never at the rate seen in Melbourne. Indeed, the Melbourne results stood at more than three times those of the highest estimates of Moody's early crusades in both the United States and Great Britain.[9] In an interview during the Mission,

---

4. *Spectator*, 23rd May 1902, 747.
5. Martin, *Apostle of Certainty*, 154.
6. Martin, *Apostle of Certainty*, 144.
7. Martin, *Apostle of Certainty*, 162.
8. Martin, *Apostle of Certainty*, 192.
9. Darrell Paproth calculates the high and low estimates of the converts in Moody's early mission work in the major cities he visited, with the highest estimate being 49,500 in a total of 76 weeks, for an average of 651 converts. This is compared with 2,160 converts each week in Melbourne ("Revivalism in Melbourne," 156).

Torrey claimed that the event was as fruitful as anticipated and that he had never seen a more responsive audience anywhere.[10] The *Southern Cross* was calling for the Mission to be repeated in 1903 and, by March that year, sixty centers were each holding services with at least 250 people, seeking to recapture the impact that had been experienced in 1902.[11] The absence of keynote speakers of renown and a lack of the same degree of organization, though, resulted in far fewer people being drawn.

Conversions in 1902 undoubtedly included those whose faith was reinforced but also those who were thoroughly transformed. The positive testimony of initial change was evidently enhanced by much longer-term impact, as seen in examples within Chapters 4 and 5. Notably, too, the conversion of businessman, Reg Nicholson, led to a fifteen-year Pacific mission at Vella Lavella in the Solomon Islands resulting in claims of the overthrow of its witchcraft and cannibalism, and the Christianization of its entire population. Vella Lavella already had twenty-three churches, 7,000 attendees and 1,450 Sunday School participants by 1913.[12] Also, when Torrey had publicly accused an interjector of high treason against Heaven's king in an Exhibition Building service, this government engineer was soon to come to faith. He spent a restless night before returning to confront Torrey and object to his claim. "The denial of a fact cannot alter the fact," came Torrey's reply which was followed by quotations from the New Testament and then the conversion of the engineer. Upon encountering Robert Harkness eighteen years later, he indicated that he remained a committed Christian.[13]

But what might we make of the resultant impact of the Mission on the city of Melbourne itself and then on subsequent revivals seen internationally?

---

10. *Southern Cross*, 23rd May 1902, 621.

11. *Southern Cross*, 30th May 1902, 647, and 20th March 1903, 265. Seizing momentum from 1902, albeit without an international keynote speaker of renown to attract significant media interest, *The Age* newspaper in Melbourne published notice of this new Simultaneous Mission (13th March 1903, 4). A similar advertisement was promoted in *The Herald*, 13th March 1903, 4.

12. Harkness, *The Man*, 119–20; *Bendigo Advertiser*, 21st August 1913, 5. Harkness shows that Reg Nicholson's ministry in Vella Lavella became the subject of a Methodist movie, *The Transformed Isle*, in 1924. Upon his arrival at the island on which cannibalism was practiced, Nicholson had shunned the offer of a revolver with the claim that the Bible would be his only defence. Medical support was provided initially, some four years before Nicholson's first convert, Bula. Nicholson reported to Torrey that witchcraft became outlawed at Vella Lavella and that the whole island had converted to Christianity.

13. Harkness, *The Man*, 56.

Social Impact

Anecdotal reports of the effect of the Mission on businesses were readily published. Melbourne event chair, S. Pearce Carey, alleged that theater owners had been claiming that "if the Mission continued much longer they would [have been] compelled to shut their doors."[14] A local constable had apparently stated that, "since the Mission opened in his district, he and his fellow-policemen had nothing to do."[15] It was claimed, too, that Torrey's impact upon the honesty of businessmen had been such that "signs were taken down [and] where goods were marked 'all silk,' they were changed to read 'half silk and wool.' Prices were lowered, according to their honorable intention, and hearts were changed."[16] Such short-term shifts observed across the city were, however, a precursor to some more notable social impact in the year following.

Subsequent to a national census being taken in the 1901 year of Australian federation, the Victorian Year Book provided statewide statistics of social importance on an annual basis. Some of these are also available for the former colony of Victoria in years prior to 1901. While the effect of the Mission on social transformation was seemingly short-lived, several modest patterns of note emerged at the time. These necessitate cautious interpretation due to a small sample size of yearly comparisons. Impact is also somewhat diluted by the use of Victoria-wide data, given the Mission's primary focus in the city of Melbourne and selected regional towns. Nevertheless, comparison with Piggin and Linder's observations regarding changes beyond 1959 (see Chapter 1) warrant similar examination of earlier social differences.

Firstly, the number of arrests for drunkenness show relatively high figures for 1900 and 1901 after a decline in the 1890s which had been characterized by financial hardship caused by a general economic depression. A 1902 decrease in arrests for drunkenness may well have been due to the Simultaneous Mission which could also have accounted for a further decrease in 1903 (just months after the event), despite an evident upsurge thereafter.

---

14. *Southern Cross*, 10th September 1902, 32.
15. *Southern Cross*, 16th May 1902, 581.
16. *Institute Tie* 1907, 193.

Table 7.1 Arrests for Drunkenness 1901–1905		
Year	Arrests (Per 1,000 People)[17]	Comparison
1900	13.31	
1901	14.43	+1.12
1902	12.00	−2.43
1903	10.45	−1.55
1904	11.50	+1.05
1905	11.92	+0.42

Births outside marriage ('illegitimate,' as they were termed at the time) decreased slightly from 5.58 as a percentage of births in 1901 to 5.50 in 1902.[18] One might, however, look to early 1903 for any birth statistics impacted by the events of April 1902 or later. An increase to 5.73 was nevertheless noted, although this would also account for pregnancies that began well after the Mission.[19] The 1904 figure was also 5.73%[20] and a slight drop to 5.61% was observed in 1905.[21] A further breakdown of monthly or quarterly figures is not available, meaning that short-term impact is difficult either to measure or interpret. Furthermore, any determination as to whether Mission attendees would have been more or less likely than others to give birth to children within marriage is speculative at best.

Divorce rates, however, decreased from 6.04 per 10,000 married couples in 1902[22] to 5.60 in 1903[23] before increasing to 7.81 in 1904.[24] A delay of one or more years was necessary for each permissible divorce category to take effect under then-current legislation. This may have suggested that the lower 1903 figure, by comparison with 1902, was impacted by the Mission, although its beneficial effect, if any, was clearly short-lived.

In considering criminal activity, one might look to arrests for crimes committed against people and property in Victoria at the time. Despite property-related crimes showing no significant pattern of change, a reduction in other serious crimes was observable from 1902 and 1903, with

---

17. McLean, *Victorian Year Book 1902*, 108; Drake, *Victorian Year Book 1905*, 397.
18. McLean, *Victorian Year Book 1902*, 175.
19. W. McLean, *Victorian Year Book 1903*, 202.
20. W. McLean, *Victorian Year Book 1904*, 346.
21. Drake, *Victorian Year Book, 1905*, 345.
22. McLean, *Victorian Year Book 1903*, 296.
23. McLean, *Victorian Year Book 1904*, 308.
24. Drake, *Victorian Year Book 1905*, 394.

a noticeable 8% drop in overall arrests in the second of these years. Of course, given that the Mission concluded well into 1902, figures for that year may be difficult to interpret, but some positive impact of the Mission upon crimes against people seems likely.

Table 7.2 Arrests for Crimes Against People & Property 1901–1905					
Year	Arrests	% Change	Against the Person	% Change	Against Property
1901[25]	27,568		1139		2,378
1902[26]	26,402	-4.2%	964	-15.4%	2,649
1903[27]	24,268	-8.1%	930	-3.5%	3,014
1904[28]	26,036	+7.3%	914	-1.7%	2,639
1905[29]	26,055	+0.1%	927	+1.4%	3,049

Should sustained delivery of the Mission have been possible for churches at the time, one wonders whether prolonged social impact would have eventuated. It is perhaps unrealistic to imagine that the energy and resources required could continue to have been invested. To what extent would the churches themselves have been capable of maintaining perpetual volunteer recruitment required and the ongoing invitation of the city's unchurched inhabitants? Irrespective of what *might* have happened, the social impact that *did* eventuate was observed only briefly and potentially attributable to just four weeks of concentrated evangelism. Nevertheless, the associated social changes observed have rarely been replicated.

The Growth of Local Churches

The 1901 mission in England had reached 200,000 people per day during its initial phase from 27th January to 5th February, even if conversion claims of half that total number were largely overstated.[30] Church impact there was modest, however, with annual growth of 0.44% in Wesleyan Methodist

---

25. Coghlan, *Statistical Account 1901–1902*, 701.
26. McLean, *Victorian Year Book 1902*, 111.
27. McLean, *Victorian Year Book 1903*, 312.
28. McLean, *Victorian Year Book 1904*, 325.
29. Drake, *Victorian Year Book 1905*, 409.
30. Tidball, "A Work so Rich in Promise," 94.

churches in 1901, growing to 1.81% in 1902 and reverting to 1.11% in 1903.[31] In noting similar growth rates in other denominations, Derek Tidball observes that the evangelism adopted had become a matter of preaching to the converted, bemoaning the continued use of such a method many decades later. Were local results to be stronger, one might expect Tidball's assessment of the Mission's potential to be less pessimistic. Was the situation in Victoria in 1902 comparable?

At the conclusion of the Melbourne Mission, only modest growth was reported for the Presbyterians and negligible change for the Congregational movement. Slight growth in the former was principally confined to inner Melbourne churches and some regional Victorian congregations directly visited by the missioners, although the Hawthorn Presbyterian church near to where Torrey preached during the suburban services reported the addition of ninety new members during the Mission.[32] The Presbyterians' 10,442 members in Melbourne in 1900 grew to 11,089 by 1902 but dropped to 10,181 the following year. The city's Congregational churches, however, showed little change in membership between 1900 and 1902, despite the Mission. These indicators appeared to be resembling patterns observed in the churches of London the previous year. Several doubts were quickly expressed as to whether a substantial impact would be seen in churches,[33] even though many had reason for earlier optimism when choosing to invest resources into the outcome. The minimal growth for some was, however, far from a universal occurrence.

One person noted that the 125 adults who he had seen respond in a suburban mission had been carefully followed up, with more than forty new members joining one church as a result.[34] One Congregational church was said to have quickly inducted thirteen new members.[35] In such instances, the coordination of the Mission had been a significant factor in ensuring not only its success as an event but, importantly, its effective follow up of new Christians. These were typically connected to local churches almost immediately. *The Argus* reported on results at the suburban venues.

> *The inquirers' cards, giving names and addresses, and the churches with which the converts would like to be associated, have to be sent*

---

31. Tidball, "A Work so Rich in Promise," 97.
32. *Punch*, 5th June 1902, 7.
33. *Southern Cross*, 16th May 1902, 593.
34. *Southern Cross*, 16th May 1902, 593.
35. *Southern Cross*, 10th September 1902, 32.

to the mission office for assortment before being despatched to their destination. Already there is a large file of these cards at the office, representing many hundreds of names. They are being dealt with as they come in.[36]

Baptist churches had reported little more than 2% growth to 6,296 members in the state by November 1901,[37] whereas this increased by 6.7% in the year of the Mission[38] before reducing to an increase of just 0.9% by the end of 1903.[39] The increase of 301 children in Sunday Schools in 1902 prompted the Baptists' Sunday School committee to report the following.

> The Simultaneous Mission had quickened the interest and strengthened the spiritual life of scholars and teachers, while at the same time it had daily added to the church those who had been halting between two opinions.[40]

The impact upon ministry to children at the time was also observed in the Christian Endeavor movement. Progress in the state's junior societies was noteworthy in the year following the Melbourne Mission, with 173 of these registered at the mid-year census accommodating 2,575 young people in 1902, an increase of 86 on the previous year.[41] By 1903, this number had increased to 211 societies and a further 1,534 members,[42] with greater numbers counted than those registering.

The growth of the Wesleyan Methodists was substantial, despite merging with other streams of Methodism on 1st January 1902.[43] Of course, Methodist statistics are difficult to analyse prior to 1902 due to the need to utilize separate reports for each Methodist tradition. Figures for Melbourne, too, included regions considered rural at the time. These outlying areas of Melbourne were less likely to have been directly impacted by the Simultaneous Mission. Official statistics concerning the significant growth

---

36. *Argus*, 21st April 1902, 6.
37. *Age*, 22nd November 1901, 8, cf. *Herald*, 16th November 1900, 4.
38. *Age*, 21st November 1902, 6.
39. *Argus*, 10th November 1904, 5.
40. *Age*, 21st November 1902, 6.
41. *Weekly Times*, 20th September 1902, 24. One society was believed to have increased its membership by fifty people as a direct and immediate result of the mission (*Southern Cross*, 10th September 1902, 32).
42. *Bendigo Independent*, 7th October 1903, 4.
43. *Age*, 1st January 1902, 5.

had adjusted for the new reporting method, although this was apparently not the case in all district calculations included in the Methodist *Spectator*.[44]

Writing on the 1902 growth in February of the following year, though, William Fitchett, editor of the *Southern Cross* newspaper and the outgoing Methodist president, noted that the Methodist movement had welcomed 614 new members and 5,000 junior members statewide, as a result of the influence of the Melbourne Mission.[45] Whereas there were 30,674 members in 1901, the growth by 614 represented a 2.0% increase to 31,288 in 1902,[46] noting that figures were reported in September after the Mission had concluded in May. The number of members increased the following year as more became eligible. The number grew by a further 1,440 to reach 32,728 by the end of 1903,[47] representing a 4.6% increase. Paproth notes that such statewide increases would not all have included professions of faith resulting from the Melbourne Mission, but nevertheless provided some measurable correlation with its success.[48] Similar large increases were once again observed statewide several years later following the Melbourne Mission conducted by Chapman and Alexander in 1909. This later event capitalized on the initial momentum generated by the 1902 visit (and subsequent mission activity) and saw 1,650 new adult members added and with a further 1,205 in 1910, representing 4.7% and 3.3% growth, respectively.[49]

---

44. A report in *The Spectator* suggested the Melbourne South region had added 1,032 members in 1902, with these Methodist figures appearing to compare only to the Wesleyan figures from 1901 (28th November 1902), 1761.

45. *Bendigo Advertiser*, 25th February 1903, 5.

46. *Annual Pastoral Address 1903*, 139.

47. The 1903 increase had been reported as 1,505 due to an error which was later amended (*Minutes of the Methodist Church* 1905, 45).

48. Paproth, *Revivalism in Melbourne*, 159.

49. *Ballarat Star*, 2nd March 1911, 2. The increases in 1909 and 1910 (aided by the 1902 experience) compared with modest increases of less than 1.5% in the years before and after this impact.

Table 7.3 Methodist Increases 1901–1905						
Year	Methodists Vic./Tas.	Increase	%	Methodists Melbourne	Increase	%
1901	30,674			9,241		
1902	31,288	614	2.0	9,954	713	7.7
1903	32,728	1,440	4.6	10,264	310	3.1
1904	33,091	363	1.1	10,309	45	0.4
1905	33,847	756	2.3	10,695	386	3.7

Examining statistics only within the Melbourne area shows the more immediate impact of the 1902 Mission where it was experienced most directly. An additional 713 persons in 1902 alone represented a 7.7% increase (with 1901 data comprising that from each pre-merger Methodist tradition and comparable 1902 data including all figures for the united Church). The Melbourne increase was despite some corresponding decreases in other regions, noting that membership growth had been static prior to 1902. Of course, the greater statewide increase of 1903 partly reflected work invested into the ongoing follow-up and recruitment of new members from among the 2,279 'members on trial' in 1902.[50] These delayed results were complemented by many early converts from mission activity in regional towns which had occurred later than that experienced in Melbourne. With these increases perhaps recalling the early 1902 anticipation of "thousands" entering the Kingdom,[51] the annual pastoral address of the Methodist union in early 1903 included an ecstatic assessment of the growth.

> *In every direction we have an advance, and from every district there comes reports of an increased earnestness and zeal which greatly encourage us . . . The good work, so well begun, has spread from city to city . . . and our churches are all enriched with the gracious gains. To those who have come into our fellowship in the past year we send our welcome. We joy over you.*[52]

To realize the vision of such impact within the churches, however, it was well understood that more work would be needed beyond the Mission.

---

50. The 1903 increase had been reported as 1,505 due to an error which was later amended: *Minutes of the Methodist Church 1905*, 45.

51. *Annual Pastoral Address 1902*, 154.

52. *Annual Pastoral Address 1903*, 139–40.

> *If the fruits of the late Mission are to be fully harvested, and the number of souls declared for God in those meetings secured and woven into church life, then something must be done to make the services of the Church less formal, and of a brighter and more exhilarating character. I believe it to be the desire of all Christians that the Church and its services should be a true reflection of what Christianity really is – the most noble and blessed state of existence possible for any person to live. Let us knock down-the walls of exclusiveness, make the seats free to all and get some of the old-time fire into our worship.*[53]

Revival in 1902?

Piggin and Linder certainly raise the possibility that global revival activity may well have begun in Melbourne.[54] Also, Joseph Nicholson, President of the National Christian Citizens' League at the time of the Mission, had suggested that the four weeks of evangelistic activity principally sought the salvation of individuals, the unification of Christians, and the salvation of society through the application of Christian principles,[55] thus broadly referencing the revival components detailed in Chapter 1, even if not all conversions were absorbed into churches.

Torrey himself considered revival to have come in 1902, but only to have touched particular parts of the world.[56] Historian, Edwin Orr, later concluded that the common source was the proliferation of "little prayer meetings" emerging in such locations.[57] H. R. Jackson's overview of churches during the early years of the twentieth century contains a blunt assessment concerning the question of "whether the long-awaited revival was in progress," asserting: "It was not."[58] So, could revival have been in existence globally, even perhaps locally? To what extent might Melbourne have been either a source or a sample of what was being observed elsewhere?

---

53. *Spectator*, 6th June 1902, 830.
54. Piggin and Linder, *The Fountain of Public Prosperity*, 530.
55. *Argus*, 19th May 1902, 7.
56. *Institute Tie* 1907, 186.
57. Orr, *Evangelical Awakenings*, 98.
58. Jackson, *Churches and People*, 58. Jackson also doubts the increase in church attendances clearly in evidence.

From Local to Global Revival

Writing in 1905, Davis claimed that the noted then-recent revivals of England and Wales had their origins in the 1902 Melbourne Mission.[59] The Mission was itself likened to the Ulster revival of 1859 due to its intensity of preparatory prayer.[60] Attributing the Melbourne success to the 1898 prayer in Chicago he was also aware, from an interview with Torrey, of the local prayer 'bands' and 'unions' whose efforts pre-dated that time.[61] For Davis, though, the direct connection to Torrey of three years of regular praying until 2 a.m. on Sundays was compelling, with 300 in prayer weekly at the Moody Bible Institute showing a passion for "a great revival of religions as had stirred the nations in past generations."[62]

Torrey later concluded that reports of the Melbourne event that had spread internationally "resulted in a wonderful work of God in the leading cities of England, Scotland and Ireland," with the 1904–5 Welsh Revival coming in a similar way, that is, through prayer.[63] The *Missionary Review of the World* published an account of Torrey's first service in London following his post-Australian visit to India. It noted the existence of the prayer circles in Melbourne and their importance in stimulating a similar work in London.[64] Two years later, it observed that, over some four or five years a "succession" of religious awakenings had begun in Melbourne, with the work in Wales being "no doubt in part traceable to Mr. Torrey's campaign."[65] Torrey's *Institute Tie* agreed, stating: "The world-wide revival for which we have been so long praying seems to have begun in Australia."[66] Torrey also stated that the ease of modern communication meant that a revival in Australia could enable a global awakening and that the world now stood on the threshold of one of history's greatest periods for the Church.[67] Davis linked Torrey to the Welsh Revival when noting its association with his Wales visit: "Many persons do not doubt that the Torrey revival campaign at Cardiff in

---

59. Davis, *Torrey and Alexander*, 9.
60. *Missionary Review* 1903, 803.
61. Davis, *Sunday Strand* 1905, n.p.
62. Davis, *Torrey and Alexander*, 11.
63. Torrey, *The Power of Prayer*, 49.
64. *Missionary Review* 1903, 220.
65. *Missionary Review* 1905, 300.
66. *Institute Tie* 1902, 431.
67. Williamson, *A Great Revival*, 81.

August 1904 was largely responsible for the wonderful religious awakening which immediately after the crusade swept South Wales like a cyclone."[68]

Warren's own wife had attended England's Keswick Convention after the couple relocated to London following the 1902 Mission, telling of the prayer circles in Melbourne.[69] Warren himself claimed, upon returning to England, that the awakening which had impacted the British colonies "started in Melbourne and spread through a large part of Eastern Australia."[70] By 1904, 30,000 similar prayer circles had been established throughout England, Wales, Scotland and Ireland,[71] by which the revival in Wales was ushered in under the leadership of Evan Roberts. This was foreseen by Torrey who perhaps spoke prophetically on the opening night of the Melbourne Mission.

> *I believe that the world-wide revival has begun. We have heard tonight that the big revival was coming in Australia. It is coming to all the earth . . . I thank God that I live in the year 1902. Brethren, I say it from no confidence of my own, but because I believe I have heard the voice of God, that you and I are to see one of the mightiest movements of the Church of Jesus Christ on the earth."[72]*

In connection with Torrey's Cardiff visit, a letter was sent by Seth Joshua who referred to kneeling next to Evan Roberts while he experienced the power of God. Joshua continued: "The power of God came down in Cardiff too. When we left, the meeting went right on without us and they went on for a whole year – meetings every night and multitudes converted."[73] Torrey did not meet Roberts directly but corresponded with him later that year, telling of the years of prayer for a worldwide revival which was now in evidence.

> *I have heard with great joy of the way in which God has been using you as the instrument of his power in different places in Wales. I simply write you this letter to let you know of my interest in you, and to tell you that I am praying for you. I have been praying for a long time that God would raise up men of his own choosing in different parts of the world, and mightily anoint them with the Holy Spirit,*

68. Davis, *Twice Around the World*, 106.
69. Davis, *Torrey and* Alexander, 16.
70. *Missionary Review* 1903, 200.
71. Davis, *Torrey and* Alexander, 16.
72. *Southern Cross*, 18th April 1902, 434.
73. Whittaker, *Great Revivals*, 95.

> *and bring in a mighty revival of his work. It is so sadly needed in these times. I cannot tell you the joy that has come to my heart as I have read of the mighty work of God in Wales ... May God keep you humble and fill you more and more with his mighty power. I hope that some day I may have the privilege of meeting you.*[74]

Writing of her first-hand connection both to the Welsh Revival and Evan Roberts, Jessie Penn-Lewis noted that Roberts had himself been praying for revival for eleven years,[75] this period post-dating the origins of the Melbourne 'Prayer Band.' Penn-Lewis noted, too, the influence in Wales of Melbourne's prayer circles as stories reached the 1902 Keswick gathering prompting her to ask: "If a city may be thus girdled with prayer, why not the world?"[76] The impact of the Melbourne revival was indeed also felt beyond Wales.

Revival in Asia can be traced to the impact of Melbourne on Pandita Ramabai's Mukti ('salvation') mission in India from 1905.[77] The mission began operating in the late nineteenth century but Ramabai sent her assistant, Minnie Abrams, to Melbourne along with her daughter after convincing them to search out the keys to the revival there.

> *"They have had a revival over in Australia and I would like to know how they got it. We must have a revival; you see our girls have turned to the Lord Jesus Christ, they have turned from idols, but they lack the power of God in their lives, and they lack that sense of the sinfulness of sin in order to give up sin; they haven't a sense of sin. We must have a mighty revival in Mukti, otherwise how can we bring the heathen to Christ? I wish you would go over to Australia and search out how they got it."*[78]

As a result of their visit, Mukti began operations in Melbourne in 1903. Abrams also concluded that the Prayer Band of John MacNeil had been responsible for the organizational efforts that resulted in the visits of Torrey and Alexander. She then inspired Ramabai to call her own mission to prayer, with seventy, and later five hundred, forming a "band" of their

---

74. Evans, *The Welsh Revival*, 121.
75. Penn-Lewis, *Awakening in Wales*, 37.
76. Penn-Lewis, *Awakening in Wales*, 18–19.
77. Despite acknowledging and earlier Pentecostal experience in India, Ivan Satyavrata attests that South Asian Pentecostalism's beginnings at the Mukti Mission are uncontested ("Contextual Perspectives," 204).
78. Abrams, "The Recent Revival," 8.

own. They sought an eventual "outpouring of the Holy Spirit,"[79] and, with the encouragement of stories from Wales, the number of prayer circles increased from 70 to 700 in just a few months.[80]

Abrams' book *The Baptism of the Holy Ghost and Fire* then influenced Dr. Willis C. Hoover who corresponded with her and with other leaders of international revivals.[81] Hoover assembled a small group in Chile to pray daily for revival. After being expelled from their Methodist churches when they began to speak in tongues and experience visions, they formed the Methodist Pentecostal Church (M.P.C.) and rapidly planted new congregations throughout the nation.[82] Eventually spawning thirty Pentecostal denominations, the M.P.C. was also involved in reaching neighbouring Argentina and Bolivia with the Gospel.[83]

The awakening in Wales also perpetuated its Melbourne influence elsewhere in India, at Khassia Hills and beyond, through the work of Welsh missionaries who also impacted Madagascar.[84] Welsh Christians were known to be praying for Khassia which experienced a revival in 1905 in which significant conversions and healing miracles occurred.[85] Stories of the revivals in Wales and India were then carried to Korean Christians by Dr. Howard A. Johnston, stimulating local prayer and, in 1907, the Pyongyang Revival in which a ten-day conference precipitated extraordinary prayer and confession.[86] Resultant growth in the Korean Church from a small minority to some 300,000 people led to the Edinburgh Missionary Conference of 1910 hailing the impact as a "genuine Pentecost."[87]

Torrey's Influence on Pentecostalism

Whatever the Pentecostal impact in Korea or at Mukti, Pentecostalism was itself only just emerging as a global phenomenon. F. Dale Bruner asserts, however, that the proximity of Torrey's ministry to the emergence

79. Abrams, "The Recent Revival," 8.
80. Dyer, *Pandita Ramabai*, 101.
81. Anderson, *An Introduction*, 64.
82. Synan, "Missionaries," 48–9.
83. Anderson, *An Introduction*, 67.
84. Anderson, "Pandita Ramabai," 37.
85. Dyer, *Revival in India*, 30.
86. Shaw, *Global Awakening*, 40.
87. Shaw, *Global Awakening*, 45–6.

of Pentecostalism made his influence greater than it otherwise might have been, with his teachings on the subsequence of Spirit Baptism making him "a kind of John the Baptist figure for later Pentecostalism."[88] For Chant, Torrey was indirectly responsible for the emergence of the earliest Pentecostal churches due to his focus on the receipt of Spirit Baptism.[89] This was for an empowerment of service, rather than for holiness as had been advocated by Charles Finney (who nevertheless impacted Torrey through his revivalist preaching, biography, and *Lectures on Revivals of Religion*).[90]

An emboldened Torrey, in turn, directly influenced several noted European Pentecostal leaders such as T. B. Barratt in Norway[91] and Johannes Rietdijk in Belgium.[92] Reports of international revivals, including that in Wales in 1904–5, reached Germany. The subsequent visit of Torrey there in 1906, preaching on Baptism in the Spirit, accelerated the evangelistic impact already connected to local prayer meetings and existing mission efforts.[93] Torrey's connection with Lutheran ministers in Poland also facilitated the growth of neo-Pietistic ideas which stimulated the earliest Pentecostal influences there.[94]

Similarly, early American Pentecostal leader, Charles Parham, was influenced by the writings of Torrey and, in particular, his expectation of a worldwide revival that would precede the return of Christ.[95] Parham accepted the possibility that Spirit Baptism, inclusive of the gift of tongues, was given to accelerate global evangelization.[96] This emerging view nevertheless began to be reassessed by Pentecostals by the end of 1908 as the Pentecostal revival at Azusa Street, Los Angeles, began to subside.[97] Two years earlier, it had also seen a Welsh influence.

During the Welsh Revival, Evan Roberts was befriended by Joseph Smale, a Los Angeles pastor originally from England. Upon his return

88. Bruner, *A Theology*, 45.
89. Chant, *The Spirit of Pentecost*, 92.
90. Davis, *Torrey and Alexander*, 27.
91. Schmidgall, *European Pentecostalism*, 18.
92. Schmidgall, *European Pentecostalism*, 114.
93. Schmidgall, *European Pentecostalism*, 126; Anderson, *An Introduction*, 88. Nienkirchen asserts that Torrey "sowed the seeds of the Pentecostal movement in Germany" (*A. B. Simpson*, 27).
94. Schmidgall, *European Pentecostalism*, 203.
95. Faupel, *The Everlasting Gospel*, 167.
96. Faupel, *The Everlasting Gospel*, 167; Anderson, *An Introduction*, 33–4.
97. Faupel, *Everlasting Gospel* 228.

home, Smale was convinced that revival could come to Los Angeles as it had to Wales.[98] Frank Bartleman, chronicler of the Azusa Street revival and frequent visitor to Smale's congregation, made contact with Roberts concerning the need for revival, receiving the first of several letters from him. Roberts advised Bartleman to "congregate the people together who [were] willing to make a total surrender" in prayer and waiting.[99] Smale's subsequent insistence on fifteen weeks of daily prayer for revival at the First Baptist Church which he pastored led to his board asking him to cease or depart. Smale resigned but was then urged to commence a new church by many of his congregation members.[100] Continued prayer for an awakening led to manifestations of people speaking in tongues after having attended the early Azusa Street revival services of William Seymour, resulting in Smale believing his prayers were indeed being answered.[101]

Pentecostal origins during this first decade of the twentieth century, therefore, were seemingly connected to an existing worldwide revival, rather than precipitating one. If so, the emerging expressions of Pentecostalism might collectively be thought of as being part of a continuing global awakening. Convergent influences may be traced to local prayer meetings in multiple worldwide centers of evangelistic activity, several of which had been touched by Torrey, inspired by his earlier Melbourne visit.[102] Bartleman, unaware of any such pre-history in Melbourne, claimed that Azusa Street was "rocked in the cradle of little Wales; it was brought up in India, following; becoming full grown in Los Angeles later."[103] This international revival phenomenon was later institutionalised through the establishment of networks and denominations such as the Assemblies of God (also

98. Bartleman, *Azusa Street*, 20.

99. Bartleman, *Azusa Street*, 15.

100. Robeck Jr., *Azusa Street Mission*, 58–9.

101. Robeck Jr., *Azusa Street Mission*, 198. Though somewhat more reserved in his support of the revival, Smale's later rebuke of apparent excesses led to the departure of congregation members who commenced a new church community while Smale, ironically somewhat like Roberts in Wales, faded into relative obscurity as revival abated.

102. J. Edwin Orr identifies the first decade of the twentieth century as a Fifth Great Awakening, following the better known First Great Awakening of the 1730s and 40s in Britain and the American colonies, the Second Great Awakening in early 19th century America, and the less well-established and so-called third and fourth awakenings of the 1830s and 40s, and the late 1850s, respectively. Orr contends that the Azusa Street revival, though central to the globalization of Pentecostalism, was an indirect and later product of a worldwide phenomenon of evangelistic impact (*Evangelical Awakenings*, 97).

103. Bartleman, *Azusa Street*, 19.

known in Australia as the Australian Christian Churches). The development of any such Pentecostal awakening had, however, been influenced by revival occurrences in nations that predated its presumed 1906 beginning. The revival in Melbourne predated them all.

Study Questions

1. What is your impression of the number of conversions at the Mission and the way that they compare with results by Torrey and Moody in other cities?

2. Consider the story of Reg Nicholson and his impact on Vella Lavella in the Solomon Islands. In what way does your own service of Christ demonstrate missionary zeal? How might Nicholson's story inspire a life of total devotion?

3. Is there any reason why the 1902 Mission might have accounted for a reduction in divorces, in crimes against people, or in arrests for drunkenness? Conversely, are these decreases purely coincidental? Are there other factors that might have influenced the social impact observed at the time?

4. How would you interpret the short-term growth noticed in the Methodist and Baptist churches in 1902 and 1903? Why do you think growth was not at a similar level in all participating denominations? Does the growth of 1902 provide us with any lessons today?

5. How do the elements of the 1902 Mission compare with the features of revivals identified in Chapter 1? Was the 1902 event a revival and is it in any way reproducible?

6. To what extent did the events in Melbourne in 1902 stimulate revival in other parts of the world? Alternatively, were the local revivals elsewhere the culmination of many years of momentum that had built globally? To what extent were they perhaps sovereign and coincidental works of God?

7. In what way was Torrey's 1902 Melbourne visit a key to the global emergence of Pentecostalism in 1906? Was the Welsh revival of 1904–5 an intermediary step in this development?

8.

Revival Revisited

What Melbourne Offered the World in 1902

Hawthorn was one of the suburban centers used in the first weeks of the Mission, and the one at which Torrey spoke. The 21st of April meeting held there was described as "a more decided and unmistakable manifestation of spiritual power" than any held to that date. One observer noted that "if any force can reach the unconverted among us it must be addresses like this, convincing argument lighted up by examples and illustrations from real life, with pungent and moving appeals, and all pervaded by the power of the Holy Ghost." It was claimed that "one after another rose in quick succession" in response to an appeal to hearers to commit their lives to Christ. Torrey asked those in the front rows to make room for people coming forward to be counselled and prayed with by ministers in a scene reminiscent of "an old-fashioned Methodist revival."[1]

Torrey was, at that stage, yet to take his revivalism to New Zealand, Ceylon (now Sri Lanka), India, England, Ireland, Scotland and Wales. Geoffrey Treloar demonstrates that Torrey's lengthy series of international mission destinations uniquely positioned him as the first genuinely global revivalist.

> Well-established networks and cultural flows made "Australia 1902" the springboard to the first world-encircling campaign of its kind in the history of Christianity. If a sustained mission along modern lines is the criterion, it made Torrey the first global revivalist.[2]

1. *Southern Cross*, 5th June 1902, 13–14.
2. Treloar, "The First Global Revivalist," 895.

Although Torrey's unique impact was an important influence in the nations he visited, the initial impetus of the Melbourne Mission had helped to spark a chain of international revivals. The continued prayer and evangelism experienced in multiple countries built upon Melbourne's earlier example throughout the first decade of the twentieth century. This catalyzed a unique global awakening which now necessitates a reconsideration of the origins of some of its famous constituent revivals in Wales and Los Angeles.

The joint efforts of Torrey and Geil while on the early legs of their planned global tours showed an important feature of revivals, that these were not dependent upon particular personalities or styles but on a combination of factors. The complementary approaches of Torrey and Geil intersected in Melbourne, but the impact of Geil's methodical prayer planning and Torrey's continued preaching of conversion and Spirit-empowerment also assisted. These factors proceeded to generate evangelistic passion and to then prioritize its ongoing observance for some ten years beyond the Melbourne event. The synergistic work of the two evangelists, along with that of Charles Alexander, offered a unique combination of missional effectiveness that undoubtedly contributed to the success of the 1902 Simultaneous Mission. It also helped to demarcate Melbourne's revival from earlier examples patterned after those that had been conducted by Moody and others.

A Pattern of Revival for Today?

As seen in Chapter 1, important features of revivals include spiritual vitality generated by united prayer and preparation, the systematic presentation of a focused message of transformation by engaging missioners central to cultivating the impact of a biblical message, sustained evangelistic momentum and fruitfulness, and evidence of significant broader church and community impact. The preceding chapters have shown the priority of each of these factors within Melbourne's 1902 Simultaneous Mission.

Firstly, the spiritual stirring caused by divine operation within united preparation, prolonged prayer, and a commitment to ecumenism, ensured the involvement of 214 churches well before, and also during, the event. The difficulty in harnessing similar cooperation today is perhaps not due to any lack of collective will to engage. Rather, it is the commitment required that becomes a real, though understandable, challenge in an era of competing time demands, pressures, and interests. Prolonged prayer and planning is essential for encouraging spiritual revitalization accompanied by inspirational 'can do' and 'how to' preaching and leadership. This needs to be accompanied by a minimization of the dispiriting, but common, 'must do' appeals of some church leaders. As ministers face the difficulty of mobilising the sustained prayer, volunteerism, and unity that accompanies seasons of revival, a temptation exists to over-realize the importance of personal leadership impact rather than pursuing the priority of divine blessing that comes upon a united church. Leadership *is* needed, but could it not be possible to also see a collective commitment to fostering renewed spiritual vitality to encourage revival afresh? If so, would we not witness new faith commitments, sustained spiritual refreshing, the breaking of addictions, and an overcoming of various illnesses, as in past revivals? Is Chant not correct, too, when advocating the reality by which this can still become a normalized expression of a collectively-lived faith for New Testament Christians?

Secondly, evangelistic impact in 1902 occurred by building momentum through an unrelenting focus on the need for conversion, with regular appeals for people to find freedom from a life of sin. It also incorporated the importance of resultant spiritual empowerment to facilitate Christian living upon yielding to Christ. This resulted in significant numbers of conversions and also in a newfound surge in numerous local church memberships. Today, uncompromising preaching that pursues conversion is often less focused and less intentional than in the past. It is sometimes perceived to risk the alienation of its hearers, potentially resulting in would-be converts being repelled should it become too assertive or insensitive. More common, perhaps, is the sad tendency for some contemporary churches to lack conviction or authority in their messaging which is then devoid of sufficient urgency for a personal faith response. If one does not identify a crisis conversion encounter, though, will there be any certainty that conversion has taken place? Naturally, preaching is not the only means by which conversion occurs, but the Gospel still needs gospellers, whether through courses, private conversations, or lifestyle impact. The call to leaders is to adapt past revival lessons so that optimized practice, whatever its form, will still see those in need of Christ coming to faith. After all, do we not still believe in the priority of Christian salvation?

Thirdly, the preaching of Melbourne's Simultaneous Mission was accentuated by the use of a well-rehearsed methodology and inspiring and prominent leadership. The use of 'after meetings' to personalize ministry connection, the systematic approach to securing conversions, the complementary preaching styles of passionate and seasoned international speakers, and the engaging musical coordination of Charles Alexander, all assisted in generating significant responses across the four weeks of the Mission. These factors perhaps advocate for the continuing value of such church-based ministry, even though personal evangelism was also necessitated then, as now. The nature of the sermons delivered (see Appendix 2) was undoubtedly shaped to some extent by the unique interests and needs of the era. It was significantly enhanced, too, by the presence of skilled orators whose aura as international guests of renown helped to shape their influence.

Commitments to justice and global impact, as necessary as these are today, do not diminish the importance of evangelism as the third leg of the three-legged stool of church mission. Of course, evangelistic strength is enhanced by leadership, systems, and intentionality. This requires careful thought, given that Christian salvation is both an 'event' marked by justification through the Cross as well as a 'process' in which sanctification is outworked by the agency of the Spirit. This need for sanctification, too, is suggestive of the *fourth* of revival's key dimensions, the impact upon churches and broader society.

Along with measurable growth in local churches in the months following the 1902 Mission, there was a modest decrease in divorces, arrests for drunkenness, and arrests for serious crime. Of course, a 'reduction in sinful practices' (to borrow from Piggin and Linder in Chapter 1), or of lifestyles and choices antithetical to Gospel values, can be difficult to measure or to engender. To an extent, such reduction results from a sovereign work of grace. Such fruit, though expected through revival impact, also comes from the daily lived practice of New Testament Christianity. After revival's impact as an event, then, there remains the ongoing process of sustained revivalistic practice which leads people to embrace and enact ongoing Christian discipleship. Whether through faith encounters within defined periods of spiritual refreshing that we might term 'revival,' or through the ongoing and optimized work of a revivalistic and Spirit-empowered New Testament Christianity, the transformation of people and communities remains a desirable outcome for all people of faith.

A Final Word on Revival in Churches Today

For these four 'revival' features to be replicated today needs more than us merely awaiting sovereign favor. Intentional leadership, planning, and prayerfulness are significant investments into desired outcomes. Everything worth anything costs something. Faith without works is dead. The fruit of revival may, however, remain difficult to acquire due to a complex range of factors. Ecumenical effort is often sadly reduced to minimalist cooperation. Communal prayer is seldom engaged with repeated and earnest commitment outside small and familiar friendship circles. In an increasingly secular culture, evangelistic preaching and inspiring worship services are less well favored by some potential responders. Is there any hope for resurgent growth in churches and in the spread of the Gospel?

Naturally, past stories of life change remain possible outcomes today and they continue to inspire, as does the inherent transformative power of biblical Christianity. Even the present degree of openness to faith continues to encourage interest. Statistical reports affirm that 72% of Australians are at least somewhat open to a spiritual conversation, with 46% extremely, or very, open.[3] Despite allegations of antipathy or indifference towards Christianity, if not outright hostility in some quarters, one in six attend church services in Australia at least monthly,[4] and one in three do so if personally identifying with Christianity.[5] There remains a sizeable proportion of society still committed to the Christian faith, which makes advocacy for it more compelling than some might appreciate.

Of course, from within churches, sustained energy, volunteer recruitment, and passionate prayer are needed in the service of an engaging vision for a transformed society. It seems, though, that revival is first needed to mobilise the very resources that typically produce it. Greater commitment always results from spiritual rejuvenation. There exists no time like the present, then, in which to enhance the Church's efforts to promote the centrality of Christ and to communicate a vision for Christian discipleship that is thoroughly missional, prayerful, *and* life-changing. For leaders to craft conversations, events, programs, or any other vehicles for the carriage of an unchanging Gospel necessitates theological and community formation that is hopeful, powerful, and outwardly focused so as to arrest indifference.

3. McCrindle, *The Changing Faith Landscape*, 18.
4. McCrindle, *The Changing Faith Landscape*, 12.
5. McCrindle, *The Changing Faith Landscape*, 17.

Of course, the best human efforts in the service of divine empowerment will always require the undergirding priority of persistence and communal prayer. The final word, therefore, belongs to the *Southern Cross*, reflecting on the events of 1902 with timeless advice for the revisiting of revivalistic transformation and the reaffirmation of prayerfulness in our generation, just as much as in any that has gone before it.

> *Faithful men in different parts of the state were deeply impressed with the need for revival of spiritual life, and unknown to each other they made it a subject of earnest prayer. These prayers were answered, and today we give thanks to God for multitudes who have been led to listen and to embrace the Gospel of His grace.*[6]

---

6. *Southern Cross*, 10th October 1902, 1156.

Appendix 1
Timeline of Events

1835	May – European settlement of Melbourne
1836	April – First Wesleyan church service conducted in Melbourne by a regular minister
1839	November – Foundation stone laid, Melbourne's first Episcopal (Anglican) church
1851	July – The discovery of gold in regional Victoria prompting increased immigration
1877	November – Henry Varley preaches to at least 7,000 at Brighton Beach
1881	August – United Evangelistic Association offer to Charles H. Spurgeon is rejected
1883	July – Evangelization Society of Victoria (of Australasia from 1896) is established
1889	August – MacNeil's 'Prayer Band' holds its first prayer meeting in Melbourne
	October – R. A. Torrey becomes leader of the Bible Institute of the Chicago Evangelization Society (later, the Moody Bible Institute)
1891	September – Keswick Convention established in Geelong, Victoria
1892	May – First attempt to secure D. L. Moody for a mission in Melbourne is rejected
1894	March – Torrey invited to become minister of Moody's Chicago Avenue Church
1896	August – The death of MacNeil
1898	February – Chicago prayer meetings commence for world-wide revival
1899	April – Second attempt to secure D. L. Moody for a mission in Melbourne is rejected
	December – The death of D. L. Moody

Appendix 1

1901	January – Launch of England's Simultaneous Mission
	May – Parliament's opening commemorated in the Melbourne Exhibition Building
	November – Simultaneous Mission commences in Sydney
1902	January – Methodist traditions unite to form the Methodist Church of Australasia
	April – Simultaneous Mission commences in Melbourne with suburban meetings
	May – Simultaneous Mission concludes at the Exhibition Building and Town Hall
	May – Missionary and Y.M.C.A. services at the Exhibition Building
	May – Mission events conclude in Melbourne and shift to regional Victorian towns
	October – Torrey's valedictory address
1907	April – Alexander's Song Service in Melbourne
1909	April – Chapman and Alexander mission commences in Melbourne
1912	March – Chapman and Alexander mission commences in Melbourne
1959	February – Billy Graham's Southern Cross Crusade commences in Melbourne

Appendix 2
Selected Sermons

Causes of Infidelity – R. A. Torrey, Melbourne Town Hall, 25th April 1902

Southern Cross, Friday 2nd May 1902, 506b.

The profession of infidelity is very common in our day. Very frequently, when I ask men why they are not Christians, they tell me they don't believe in the Bible. I know a great many ministers – most excellent men, most learned and gifted men – think we ought not to talk about infidelity. They think we ought to deal with it by ignoring it. Well, they have a perfect right to their opinions, only I don't agree with them.

The profession of infidelity is common enough, and active enough and destructive enough in the present day to demand attention. Now it is my great privilege to have as members of my Church over in Chicago a great many men who were formerly out-and-out professors of infidelity, and these men were brought to Christ and the light through sermons which were preached against infidelity. I do not preach about infidelity because I fear for Christianity. No, Christianity is founded on a rock, and the gates of hell shall not prevail against it. Nor for fear that the Bible is in peril and needs my poor support. No, that book has stood the attacks of eighteen centuries, and is not going down in your day or mine. But there are individuals who are being injured by infidelity – there are communities being marred, if not ruined, by infidelity, and we owe it to these individuals and these communities to tell of the causes and consequences of unbelief.

Appendix 2

The first cause of infidelity is misrepresentation of Christianity by its professed disciples. I believe more infidelity is caused by this cause than any other save one. There are two kinds of misrepresentation – in our teaching, and, still more, in our living. Take the first. Much that passes for Christian teaching has in it nothing of the Christianity of the Bible, but is only a gross caricature upon it. A good deal of what passes for Christian preaching has not the Christianity of the Bible in it; the God of much preaching is not the God of the Bible; the Christ of much preaching is not the Christ of the Bible, and much of the Christian life of Christ's professed followers is not the Christian life taught by the Word of God.

But it is still more the representations of Christianity in our living that produces more infidels. Take, for instance, a man who makes great profession of Christianity, and then oppresses his employees, and grinds the utmost fraction out of them. Is it not very natural that those employees should be driven to infidelity? Here, again, is a man who professes very loudly that he is a Christian, and yet is dishonest in business. Is it any wonder that his customers are driven to infidelity? Here is a loudly professing Christian rolling in wealth and living in luxury, squandering the money God has entrusted to him, while poor starving men are turned from his door. Is it not the most natural thing in the world that his conduct should drive people to infidelity?

Mind you this, that while I say there are causes of infidelity, I do not say they are excuses. It is very foolish for a man to refuse good sovereigns because at some time or other he has been cheated with a counterfeit coin; and, in the same way, it is extremely foolish of a man to refuse to believe in God and the Bible simply because of certain spurious Christians he may happen to come across.

The second cause of infidelity is ignorance – ignorance of the Bible, of history, and of science. Almost every infidel I have come across was in the densest ignorance of the contents of the Book of books. I have never known all my life a single infidel that had a profound knowledge of the Bible, and the average infidel knows nothing about it. All he knows are a few little difficulties he has heard some infidel lecturer talk about, or has read in some infidel paper.

One night, after a meeting in Chicago, I was called to speak to a man who said he was an infidel. "Why are you an infidel?" I asked. "Because the Bible is so full of contradictions," he replied. "Please show me one," I said. "Why," he said, "it is full of them." "Then you ought to be able to show me at least one," I replied. "Well," he said, "there are some in the Psalms." I handed him my Bible, and he looked for the Psalms way over at the back part of it. I found the Psalms for him, but he couldn't point out the contradictions. "If only I had my own Bible here," he said, "I could soon show you." I asked him to meet me there at 9 o'clock with his Bible, and he promised to do so. Nine o'clock came. I came; he did not come. He had given me his address, however, but on looking it up I found that he had given me the address of a liquor saloon, and that no man of his name lived there. A few months afterwards, at a similar meeting, one of my students came to me and said that there was a man there who said that the Bible was full of contradictions. I went down to see him, and sure enough it was my friend. "You are the man that lied to me," I said. "Yes, sir," he replied, "I am."

Oh! Yes. I have tried it on thousands of infidels, and have always found that while they profess to believe that the Bible is untrue, they actually know nothing about the contents of the Book. Let me give you another instance. A bright young fellow said to me one time, "I am an infidel," and when asked, "Why?" he said, "because I don't believe that passage in the Bible where it says that Jesus Christ called fire down from heaven and consumed his foes." He really believed that the Bible said that.

The third cause of infidelity is conceit. A man finds something in the Bible that he cannot understand, and he says, "Oh! It is not true." What stupendous conceit for a man to think he can understand everything the Infinite God says. For a man to say that is to say, "I know as much as God." I get the question asked of me again and again, "Why is it that the God of our Bible, if He is almighty, allows such awful sin and suffering and misery to afflict mankind?" My dear friends, did it ever occur to you that God might have ten thousand reasons for doing a thing, when you, in your folly, could not find a single one?

Suppose I took my little girl out into the yard, and said, "See, the sun there is 92,000,000 miles away," and supposing she said, "Father, I know better; it is just back of the barn," would not my child be showing her stupidity and ignorance? She would, and so is the man who does not believe in the Bible simply because he cannot understand everything that is in it. Ah! Friends. If we had a proper humility, we would know that there are plenty of good explanations of the things we cannot understand.

The fourth cause of infidelity is sin. Sam Jones used to say, "Pull up infidelity, and you will find sin at the root of it." And I believe this is true in a large proportion of cases. You try it in your case and test it.

Appendix 2

[A man in the audience called out. "What is sin?" Dr. Torrey then responded.]

What you are doing every day, my friend. This is true in two ways. First, sinners know that the Bible condemns sin, and that it tells of penalties for sin here and hereafter. That makes a man uneasy for his sin, and to comfort himself he says, "I don't believe in the Bible, or in God." Men have many objections to the Bible, but the chief reason is because it condemns sin. I remember a man in the inquiry-room one night telling me that he was an infidel, and when I asked him why, he said, "Well, I do not see where Cain got his wife." I said, "then that is why you are not a Christian?" "Yes," he said. "If I tell you where Cain got his wife, will you become a Christian?" "Oh! I won't promise that," he said. Well, when I came to look into his case, I discovered that the trouble was not Cain's wife, but another man's wife. This is true in the second place, because sin blinds men to God's truth. Sin puts out the eyes of the soul. It is marvelous how rapidly a man goes down in unbelief when he begins to sin.

The fifth reason is resistance of the Spirit of God. The Spirit of God comes and works in your heart, and you know you ought to come to Christ, and yet you will not. You say "No" to the Spirit of God, and the Spirit of God who is the Spirit of Truth leaves you, and you get down into unbelief. There was a time in the history of most infidels, perhaps in a meeting like this, when they were touched by the Spirit of God. They knew they ought to come to Christ, yet they refused, and were forsaken by the Spirit, and drifted into infidelity.

In my first pastorate there was a very clever lawyer, who came under the deepest conviction of sin. But when he was asked to accept Christ, he said, "I know I ought to, but I will not, because it will hurt my law business." The man refused to listen to the Spirit of God because it would interfere with his law business! What was the outcome of it? The last time I went to that town that man, though he had been a lawyer of great ability, was sawing wood while his wife taught school to help keep the family. My friends, I tell you, it is a serious thing to say "No" to the Spirit of God. Oh! I beg of you, that if the Spirit of God is striving with you today you will not refuse to hear Him, but will turn to Him, and will accept Christ as your Savior.

APPENDIX 2

The Drama of Life in Three Acts - R. A. Torrey, Exhibition Building, 28th April 1902

Southern Cross, 2nd May 1902, 506d–7.

My subject tonight is the drama of life in three acts. Jesus Christ is the author of this drama. It surpasses anything ever put on the stage in conciseness, in point, in graphic delineation, in pathos, in strength of characterization, and in fullness, height, depth, and beauty of meaning.

Its dramatic personae are God, two men, and Satan. There are three acts which may be described as – First Act, Wandering; Second Act, Desolation; Third Act, The Wanderer's Return. There is a fourth act which we will not enter into tonight. We will take these acts up one by one and study them.

Act I – Wandering.

Scene 1 – A beautiful home with every provision for the comfort and enjoyment of its occupants. An elderly, white-haired father, with a face full of wisdom, nobility, kindness, and a remarkable blending of strength and tenderness, is in earnest conversation with the younger of his two sons. The boy has become tired of the restraints and dependence of home life. He longs for a life of untrammeled independence and freedom, where he can follow out the inclinations of his own sweet will. "Father," he cries, "give me the portion of thy substance that falleth to me." (Luke 15:12, R.V.) A look of deep sadness passes over the noble face of his father, but he grants the son's request and divides unto his two sons his living.

Scene 2 carries us on a few days. It represents a home-leaving. The younger son has gathered all his belongings together, put them into as portable a form as possible, and is starting out on a journey of sightseeing and pleasure-seeking into a far country. The morning is bright, the air is fragrant, the youth's heart is light. His words are blithe and gay, and little thinks he of the grand old father who watches him, with moist eyes and a lonely heart as he winds down the front lawn and out into the false and cruel world.

In these two scenes we have a picture of the beginning and growth of sin. The father of the drama represents God. The son, man wandering from God. In the first scene we have a picture of the beginning of sin. The young man desired to be independent of his father, desired to do as he pleased. This is where sin begins; in a desire to be independent of God. The desire to do as we please, not to be obliged to be always asking God what he pleases. There are many classes of sinners and many forms of sins. There are gross and there are refined forms of sins. There are low and vulgar forms of sins, and there are genteel and elegant forms of sins, but they are essentially one. All sin is alike in this. It is man seeking to be his own master, instead of joyously acknowledging God's fatherhood and sovereignty. "Come," says the sinful heart in effect to God, let me have the portion of goods that falleth to me. Give me what is to be mine – talents, gifts, graces, and abilities. Let me take them and do as I please with them. What one pleases to do may not be very bad, as the world reckons badness – it may be something refined and moral – but the spirit of doing as we please, the spirit of unwillingness to acknowledge God's right to guide and direct us, is the spirit of sin.

You will notice that the father granted his son's request, and this is precisely the way in which God deals with men. When a man wishes to live in a measure of independence of God, God lets him do it. He gives us our talents and our means of living and enjoying life, and if we must find out the folly of living away from God and without God, by bitter experience, he lets us do it and take the consequences. God does not compel men to live in communion with, and conscious dependence upon, himself.

In the second scene, we have a picture of the growth of sin. The boy did not go away from father and home at once. His heart, it is true, had already gone into the far country, but his body still stayed at home for a few days. But a few days after, his feet went where his heart had already gone. So it is with men, when they wander from God into the far country of sin, they do not at once leave God altogether. Some sort of communion is still kept up. The man still goes to church, he thinks of God occasionally, it may be he prays to him now and then, though less and less as time passes. It is only after a time, when sin has grown in his heart, that he takes his departure altogether into the far country, gets just as far away from God as he can, thinks of God just as little as possible, and then, perhaps, begins to question whether there is any God, and then surrenders himself gradually to voices that say there is not, and at last, he boisterously asserts, "There is no God." All his thoughts are, "There is no God." (Psalm 10:4 R.V.) My friend, where are you tonight? Just starting out to have your own way, but still living in some measure in God's presence? Or are you well on your way to the far country, leaving God more and more out of your thoughts and plans and life? Or have you already reached the far country where you are living utterly without God?

Act II – Desolation.

We now come to the Second Act in the drama. We will entitle this act: 'In the Far Country,' or 'Desolation.' There are three scenes in this act. The first scene is a gay one. The young man has reached the far country. He is surrounded by hosts of bright, and splendid, and merry companions. Club parties, balls, races, theaters, champagne parties, and all conceivable forms of hilarity and pleasure, innocent and sinful, are the order of the day. The young man is having a right royal time.

The scene shifts. Hard times have struck the gay capital. Famine stalks the streets. Crowds of hungry men throng the streets, trying to catch a stray penny to starve off want. A young friend is among them. His money is gone. Fast living has used up his generous patrimony. Work is hard to find, and he begins to feel the pinch of actual hunger.

The scene shifts again. It is now a rural scene, but not an attractive one. A desolate field, a lonely carob tree, with its brown pods covered with dust from the arid land. A herd of gaunt, hungry hogs, nosing about for a stray carob bean, and our friend in ragged clothes, with hungry face and emaciated form, looking up into the carob tree, for he would fain have filled his belly with the husks that the swine did eat. Driven by hunger, but at the same time weakened by it, he wearily climbs the carob tree and shakes it. The dry husks come rattling to the ground. He hurries down, but the hungry hogs have swallowed the last bean before he reaches the ground. Again and again he tries it, with the same result, and at last sinks down in despair, starvation staring him in the face, "and no man gave unto him." The man who has sent him into the fields to feed swine leaves him to pick up his own living.

In the three scenes of this act, we have a vivid and suggestive picture of the fruits of sin. The first fruit of sin is pleasure. The young man had a good time at first. Your moral teachers will tell you that there is no pleasure in sin. I will not tell you that, for three reasons. First, you wouldn't believe me if I did. You have tried it and found pleasure in sin. Second, I know better. I know there is pleasure in sin. Third, the Bible does not say so. It says it is true that "there is no peace for the wicked," and that you know, or soon will know, to be true. But the Bible does not say there is no pleasure

Appendix 2

in sin. Indeed, it speaks of "the pleasures of sin." (Hebrews 11:25 R.V.) It is true, it says, they are only for a season," – very, very short-lived. They don't last, and one has to pay very dearly for them. It is true that the happiness found in sin is not of a noble sort, and it is soon gone, but it is happiness of a sort. Sometimes, someone has well said, "the devil is not such a fool as to go fishing without bait." The pleasures of sin are the devil's bait, but that bait always has a sharp hook in it. He is dangling it before the eyes of some of you young men and women – yes, and some of you older men and women – tonight. You bite the bait at your peril. You will have the devil's hook in your gills and soon be floundering in the devil's boat, beneath a pitiless sun, floating on the sea of a hopeless eternity.

The second fruit of sin is want. "He began to be in want." No one ever went into the far country, went away from God into sin, but he soon began to be in want. To many, this want comes in a very natural, in a very literal way, want of temporal things, want of the very necessities of life. How many men and women there are in this city tonight who want clothing to cover them and food to satisfy their hunger? They are walking these streets hungry. They have come in here – some of them – tonight, hungry. They don't know where they are to sleep tonight. And some of them once had plenty. They have good abilities. Why then this want? They have gone into the far country, they have wandered from God. The thousands of tramps that sleep with empty stomachs in lodging houses and jails tonight – what has brought them there? Almost everyone has been brought there by sin. They have been in the far country. The pleasures of sin have been followed by the want of sin. High times have been followed by hungry times.

But this is not the only way, nor the most important way in which the one who goes into the far country begins to be in want. There is other want than temporal want. There is other hunger than physical hunger. There is soul want and soul hunger. Every man who goes into the far country, every man who gets away from God will soon begin to be in want. He may have everything the body wants. Plenty of food, plenty of drink, plenty of clothing, but the deeper, more important wants of the soul will be unsatisfied. The soul will want that which is most essential for it. That for which God made it, that without which life soon becomes barren, a burden and a curse. God did not make these souls of ours for mere eating and drinking, for mere money-seeking and money-getting, for mere pleasure-seeking. God made these souls of ours for knowledge of himself, for likeness to himself, for communion with himself, for life like his own. He made them for himself, to fill them with himself.

There is such a largeness in the human soul that the world cannot fill it. God alone can fill it. Saint Augustine well said hundreds of years ago, "Lord, thou hast made us for thee, and our heart is disquieted until it resteth in thee." Without God, there is unrest, there is an aching void, there is constant and ever-increasing dissatisfaction, there is the abyss of infinite and insatiable desire. There is woe, woe, woe. Whosoever goes away from God goes into famine. Look at the wretched young man of whom Jesus Christ, in this wonderful drama, has drawn a picture as he sits there, pale and thin and hungry, with the craving of his stomach looking out of those hungry, half-crazed eyes. This is a picture of the soul away from God. A picture of your soul, and yours, and yours, and every soul in this house tonight that is away from God.

The third fruit of sin is degradation and abject slavery. "He went and joined himself to a citizen of that country, and he sent him into his fields to feed swine." To feed swine was the deepest depth of degradation for a Jew, and Jesus, by this picture, represents the awful degradation of a soul that wanders from God. It is a true picture. Who so leaves God goes into degradation and slavery. This young man got rid, it is true, of his father's guidance and control, but he became the bondman of a stranger. So it is with everyone who throws off God's paternal control. He becomes Satan's swineherd – hog tender for the devil, to put it in plain English. Each man here tonight has his choice. To be a son of God, in filial, joyous, ennobling, and abundantly rewarded obedience, or Satan's slave, in degrading, repulsive, and unrequited drudgery. Which will you choose? You must take one or the other. "I wish to be my own master," young men cry, and old men cry, "you can't." God's sons or Satan's slaves, which will it be?

Act III – *The Wanderer's Return.*

We come now briefly to the third and last Act, The Wanderer's Return. There are two scenes. The first is still the barren field. The young man has sat down, the swine are peering curiously and hungrily at him. His face is buried in his hands. He is thinking. Visions of the old home are passing through his brain. He sees the spacious house, he sees his aged father, he sees the well-loaded tables, he sees the very servants, well-clothed, well-fed, and happy. "How many hired servants of my father have bread enough to spare, and I perish with hunger?" he bitterly cries. Then he is still again. He is still thinking. Suddenly he lifts his head. And there is a new light of hope in those hungry eyes. "I will arise and go to my father," he cries, "and will say unto him," etc. (Luke 15:18-19). He springs to his feet, turns his back on husks and hogs and hunger, and steadfastly sets his face homeward and fatherward.

In this scene, we have a picture of the remedy for sin and its bitter consequences. Note the steps. He began to think. That is one of the best things any lost man can do. I have heard people say that they were not Christians, because they thought for themselves. I venture to say, for every person who is not a Christian because he thinks, I can show you ten who are not Christians because they don't think. Ah, how many there are in this audience tonight who are not Christians because you don't think, because you won't think, because you are bound not to think, because you are going through the world with your eyes shut and are determined no one shall open them for you. When something is said to make you think, you giggle and so try to drive it away, or you get up and go out. Determined, obstinate thoughtlessness is destroying millions of souls and is destroying many here tonight. And if I could only get some of you here tonight to thinking, I could get you saved.

Now, I want you to note three things. First, note what he thought about. The better lot of his father's servants. That is the thing to think about. Your miserable lot as a slave of Satan, and the better lot as a servant of God, to say nothing of a son. Note then that the second step was, he resolved, "I will," etc. "All our thinking will do no good unless it ripens into resolution," wisely said John Evans. His resolution was threefold. (1) To go to his father. That is the place to go – right to God. (2) To confess his sin. That is the way to go to God – with a confession on your lips. That is the only way for a sinner to come to God (1 John 1:9; Luke 18:13-14). To seek acceptance. He was going to seek acceptance as a servant. He got something better – welcome as a son. Thirdly, note that "he arose and came to his father." That is the final step. Just came.

We come now to the final scene of the third act. What the young man's thoughts, by the way may have been, we are not told. He may have had doubts and fears. He may have vainly wished he could fix himself up better before going home. We are not told. At all events, he wisely kept trudging on just as he was. It is near sunset. In the twilight on the crest of a hill, we see an old man standing, peering off into the distance. Many a night he has stood thus, watching for the homecoming of a loved son who never came. The boy had forgotten his father. The father had never forgotten the boy. We forget God. God never forgets us. He's watching for your return tonight. Watching with yearning heart. This time, as the aged man stands there in the same old spot, he sees a speck in the distance and he peers more eagerly. It comes nearer. It assumes the proportions and form of a man. It is not at all like the young man that left the home in the days agone. It is not the same rotund form. Not the same cheery face. Not the same fine garments. Not the same tripping gait. But those eyes, though dimmed by age, are keen by love, and beneath all this changed exterior, he knows his darling boy. "My son, my son," he cries, while the wanderer is yet a great way off. Those aged feet forget their infirmity. He runs to meet his boy. He falls upon his neck, encircles his ragged clothes with an arm of love, and kisses his sin-stained and travel-stained cheek. The boy is overwhelmed with grief, but stammers forth his confusion.

Friends, of whom have we a picture here? Of God and God's attitude toward the wanderer that returns to him. Have you wandered from God? It may not be that you are a profligate, nor an immoral man or woman, but have you wandered from God? Have you tried to live without God? Tried to live as you pleased? This parallel is for you. Come back to God tonight. There only can joy be found. There is famine, want, degradation away from him. Come home. Come just as you are. There is a welcome, a robe, a kiss, a ring, a feast awaiting you. God is waiting. Come.

Right is Right, Wrong is Wrong – W. E. Geil, Exhibition Building, 4th May 1902

Southern Cross, 9th May 1902, 552–553.

The Gospel according to Dr. Luke 17:14, as they went they were cleansed. Ten lepers! I came from the Garden of Gethsemane one summer's day, and saw a leper with his arm rotted off to the elbow. Down near the tomb of Absalom I found a leper with his foot rotted off to the ankle. Ten lepers by the roadside, and Jesus Christ coming along! I don't suppose that the lepers were in the same stage of being eaten by the leprosy. I can think of some with an arm off; I can think of some with a foot off, of some with a bright spot on the hand, and of some with a crimson glow on the forehead. They were all sorts of lepers and Jesus said to them, "Lepers, go show yourselves to the priests." What? Lepers, are they not to tarry by the roadside until the leprosy has gone? No, Jesus Christ has pronounced a most stupendous truth. Let me put that truth in my own phrasing. Listen!

Right is right and wrong is wrong. Hot or cold, young or old, clear or cloudy, saint or sinner; right is always right, and wrong is always wrong; wrong is never right and right is never wrong.

It was the business of these lepers to do just what Christ said. They must not wait to be cleansed of their leprosy. If they fail to go, they will die lepers. So, it is the business of the lepers to do what is right, leprosy or no leprosy.

Can anyone lend me a match? [Receiving and striking it]: See here this is no child's play. I am doing this now for the man who has power to think. Now, I am not going to talk about theories of combustion, nor concerning the three flames in one – the trinity of flame – that is here before you. Had I never felt fire or heat there would be two ways by means of which I might come to an understanding of the effect of heat on the human body. First, there would be the theoretical – a circuitous business; and secondly, there would be the experimental, a shorter way. I could either have the theory of the thing elaborately explained to me, or I could put my finger in the flame and find out. Now, there are two ways of finding out somewhat concerning Jesus of Nazareth and His religion. One is to sit down, put your feet up on a piano stool, and enter into a debate on the subject. The other – shorter and more satisfactory – is to come and see for yourself. These lepers might have organized themselves into a debating society, and sat down by the roadside to argue the value of the advice, and one of them might have said, "What is the use of going?" But "as they went, they were cleansed."

My friends, the first great thought of tonight's subject is this: Go upon the statement of Jesus Christ until you prove Him right, or prove Him a liar. For, remember, you are to do right tonight, whether you are a Church member or not, whether you are an atheist or not, whether you are a drunkard or not. You may be a licentious man, a cursing, swearing, godless wretch – it is your business to do right this very moment. The lepers go and, "as they went they were cleansed." They have nothing to wait for. The man who is down in the utmost depths of degradation has nothing to wait for. He must do right this instant, leprosy or no leprosy, sin or no sin, for right is right and wrong is wrong. Hot or cold, young or old, clear or cloudy, saint or sinner; right is always right, and wrong is always wrong; wrong is never right and right is never wrong.

Appendix 2

But say! That was a pretty shrewd thing that a parson did in the street of Washington one day. Do you know there are some pretty shrewd parsons about, though some people seem to think that the men who stand on the platform for God are not so shrewd or 'slick' as the men behind the counter. Well, this parson stopped a judge of the Supreme Court, and said to him, "Your Honor, do you have family worship in your home?" "No," replied the judge, "I do not, because I am not a professing Christian." "But," said the keen clergyman, "would it not be right, judge, for you to have family worship? Do you not think that it would be vastly better for the American nation if in every household under the flag family worship were observed?" "To be sure I do," replied the judge. "Well, then," said the parson, "you have admitted it is right – you do it." Ah! He has taken the ground from under the judge's feet. The judge has admitted it is right. Get away from that, if you can. Crawl out from underneath that, sir, and you are not worthy of the name of man!

The judge went home. The next morning he called the household together – servants, guests, and all – and announced, "Today we begin family worship in this house. It is right; therefore we do it." All the family wondered what he was going to do about the praying; but, after reading a chapter from the Bible, he said, "We will all repeat the Lord's Prayer." They conducted worship along these lines for two weeks; then one morning the judge said, "Before we repeat the Lord's Prayer this morning I wish to pray." And that learned jurist of the Supreme Court of America then and there asked God to forgive his sins, to save him, and to lead his family to accept the Master. As he went he was cleansed. Right is right.

"But," you say, "I have no conviction of sin." You have the conviction of fact, though. What more do you want? You know what is right. The only question is this: Is there enough of the manly spirit yet in you so that a man can appeal to you as a man, or must you be excited, or made to laugh and cry, which can be as easily done as the turning of the human hand. I want to appeal to you tonight as a man to men. I don't want to let go that power which will make you laugh and cry; but I appeal to you as men tonight, right is right and wrong is wrong. The only question is: Are you man enough to face it? The conviction of knowledge is sufficient, and every man here tonight has got that.

In a regimental prayer meeting in England – and thank God for the spirit which prevails amongst so many men in the army of your great Empire – a soldier came and stood up in cold blood – just as a soldier does things – and said, "Comrades, I am going to lead a godly life." Excited? No. Overpowering emotion? No emotion at all. It is right, therefore the soldier will do it. The man who is willing to look into the mouth of a cannon that is just about to belch forth flame and shot and death has found himself manly enough to stand up in a prayer meeting and say, "Comrades, I am going to lead a godly life." He left for his tent. In the middle of the night he awoke, and was greatly disturbed in his mind. "I made a mistake," he said to himself. "I had no conviction of sin; and yet I did it as a soldier." Next morning he received two letters – one from Washington and one from Boston. One told of the death of a young man in delirium tremens, the other of the death of a young woman in a house of ill-fame. He came again that evening to the regimental prayer meeting, and, standing up, said, "Men, I have received these two letters. Both these people are dead now, and I led them both astray." Then the tears streamed down his face. He had all the conviction of sin he could use. He had a big supply on hand right then.

You are not to wait for conviction of sin. You are to wait for nothing. Sinful men, with your sin as black as sin can possibly be, it is your business to do what is right. It is the business of the infidel to do what is right, just as it is the business of the best preacher or the holiest Church member on this Earth. Yes, right is right and wrong is wrong. Hot or cold, young or old, clear or cloudy, saint or sinner; right is always right, and wrong is always wrong; wrong is never right and right is never wrong.

The second great thought of tonight is, that if you do what is right it will cure your infidelity. A Boston doctor of divinity ... there was a noted infidel club in Boston, and a doctor of divinity said to its leader one night, "Is there anything in the Bible you can endorse?" The infidel smiled. I like to see an infidel smile – it is a good sign – and he said, "Yes, I can endorse the Sermon on the Mount." "Ah!" said the learned doctor, "then maybe you will come down to my church on Wednesday night and tell them so." "Why should I?" said the infidel. "Is it not the business of every man," replied the doctor, "to add to the sum total of righteousness in his community?"

"I will come on the condition that I have the privilege of telling the people that I don't believe in the Divinity or the Deity of Jesus, and that of the whole Bible I only undertake to endorse the Sermon on the Mount." Well, Wednesday night came; the place was packed. I think they reckoned the infidel would be engaged that night, and would not turn up; but he kept his word, and took his seat beside the minister. By and by, when he was given the opportunity, he rose and said something like this: "I came

Appendix 2

here tonight to tell you that I don't believe in the Deity and Divinity of Jesus Christ, that I do not believe in the Bible as a whole; but that I believe in the Sermon on the Mount. But as I came along, something came into my heart and spoke a peace to me I had never experienced before, and I am going to tell you now that I believe that the Sermon on the Mount and everything else in the Bible is the revealed Word of the living God, and that Jesus Christ is the Son of God." "As he went, he was cleansed." Right is right and wrong is wrong. Hot or cold, young or old, clear or cloudy, saint or sinner; right is always right, and wrong is always wrong; wrong is never right and right is never wrong.

So that, men, if you do what is right tonight, whether you feel like it or not, it is absolutely impossible that it should be wrong – right is never wrong; the only question is, "Are you man enough to grind your teeth, to turn your hands into fists, to stamp your feet and say, 'It is right, therefore I do it'"?

When Hobson – I don't say that he was the greatest hero of the Spanish American war, but he was certainly the most picturesque hero – was ready to take the Merrimac into Santiago Straits in order to sink her there to head off the Spanish fleet; when he knew that the chances were ten to one he would never come out alive, he went down into his cabin, and wrote that historical will, now in the possession of his father. This is how he began that will, "In the name of Almighty God ... Amen. For my near and distant future I leave myself without anxiety in the hands of God." People, that is the kind of stuff heroes are made of!

One of the bravest men who lost his life in our unfortunate war with Spain said, just before he left for the front, "I am not ashamed of the Gospel of Jesus Christ." And up till the time of his death he proved it by his godly life. Why is it, friends, we are ashamed to appear to be as good as we really are? God help us once and forever to be ashamed of sin, to be ashamed of the fact that we have so hardened our hearts concerning rightness and righteousness as to be able to do wrong deliberately. Oh, if there is one person here tonight who can go on doing the wrong after having had his attention drawn to the right, he ought to be ashamed of himself; but let us not be ashamed to do the right. Right is right and wrong is wrong. Hot or cold, young or old, clear or cloudy, saint or sinner; right is always right, and wrong is always wrong; wrong is never right and right is never wrong.

A celebrated preacher was taking a series of services in a New England city one time, and just after they had begun he called upon the president of the Liberal Club, which was composed of forty-five members. "See here," he said, "I want you to come to the meeting." "Why should I come?" he said. "Don't you believe that these meetings are doing good in the town? Is not the town better for them?" "Yes," admitted the president. "Well, then, if it is right to hold the meetings, you owe it as a duty to the community to attend them." "But the people would think I was giving up infidelity and getting religious." "I will fix that," said the minister. "I will block off forty-five sittings, and you come in with your infidel club, file into the seats, and when you are in I will rise up and say, 'These gentlemen are infidels – members of the Liberal Club. They have not come here to get religion, but simply because they believe that this religious movement is a good thing for the morals of the city.'"

Well, the president said he would. So they blocked off the seats, and the first night afterwards, in walked the big infidel and forty-four little infidels and settled themselves into the reserved seats. Well, do you know two or three of the infidels were converted that night, and apparently nobody was better pleased than their chieftain. He got them to come every night and each night some would be converted. When the last night came, the president shook hands with the minister, and said, "Can I see you at ten o'clock tomorrow morning?" "Yes," said he; then turning to one of the church members he winked the eye that was furthest from the infidel. But the infidel saw the wink, and remarked, "See here! I was going to ask you tomorrow morning if you thought it possible for an infidel to be converted. Now what do you mean by that wink? You don't think I am converted now, do you?" "I won't say you are converted," said the minister, "but I will say this, that if you will continue to work for the conversion of men as you have done during the last ten days, I guess you won't be unconverted long!" He did not turn up the next morning – no need to! For sixteen years that man converted had one of the largest Bible classes in his city, and was used for the conversion of hundreds of people. "As he went he was cleansed."

Remember, men, when the leprosy of sin is upon you, you are to do what God says. You are not to wait for one spot of the leprosy to be gone, you are not to wait for your sins to be removed, you are not to wait 'til you are able to quit desecrating God's day, you are to wait for nothing. Right is right and wrong is wrong. And the right thing is to come to Jesus when He says "Come!" God help you to do right tonight, and as you go you will be cleansed.

Appendix 2

And what will be the result if you are cleansed? Sympathy will come back to you again. I pity the man or the woman who has no sympathy with the man who is weak, with the woman who is down, with the multitude who are in the hard way of the transgressor. Oh, men have you lost sympathy? I met a man on the steamer, coming down from Pago Pago, who told me that he had lost faith in the world, in everybody and everything. He did not believe that there were any good people in the world, and he thought that everybody was trying to 'do' him. I pitied him. It is a dreadful thing not to believe in men; it is a dreadful thing to believe that everybody is bad and wrong; it is a dreadful thing not to have sympathy with the poor lad working his way through school, with the poor woman who rubs her finger-nails off at the wash-board to buy clothes for her children. I pity the man who has no sympathy for the brother man who staggers out of the gin palace and goes stumbling down the broad road. Ah, yes, if you go and do right this moment, as you go you will be cleansed, and sympathy will come.

It has been my custom every other summer to spend two or three months at work in the British Museum library. I was at work one summer when I came across an Arabic poem called 'The Child of Sorrow.' The story is of a young man who is unbalanced in his mind; the scene is a forest – sun getting ready to go down behind the western hills,shadows lengthening across the pasture, and so forth. It runs –

> *Through yonder dark sequestered grove*
> *I saw a moody maniac rove.*
> *With hurried step he paced along.*
> *And wildly breathed a plaintive song.*
> *"Sweetly though sing'st, poor youth," I cry.*
> *"Ha!" fierce he called, "what foe to try*
> *To flatter such a wretch as I?*
> *Too well I know how fatal they*
> *Who mean not what they seem to say.*
> *Hence, though perfidious! Hence, retire!*
> *Or dread the child of sorrow's ire!"*
> *Yet still I stayed, till my wet cheek*
> *The pity told I could not speak.*
> *'Twas then I saw his rage subside,*
> *'Twas then with altered voice, he cried,*
> *'Yes, stranger, yes, that starting tear*
> *Has told me that though art sincere.*
> *Stay if thou wilt, in welcome stay,*
> *And hear the Child of Sorrows lay.*

Oh! What a magnificent power is sympathy, how well it will soften a man; and if you are kind and sympathetic, doing the will of God as men, you will find that the sympathy you have shown will come home to roost.

Oh, God bless you men and women, let us be kind and helpful, let us have compassion and sympathy, and whatever your condition, may God help you to do the right tonight, because the right is never wrong. Now, you know absolutely what is the right thing for you to do tonight. Do it! Let me, in closing, repeat once again the statement which I have so often used tonight, and which I hope will stick in your memory for ever:-

Right is right and wrong is wrong. Hot or cold, young or old, clear or cloudy, saint or sinner; right is always right, and wrong is always wrong; wrong is never right and right is never wrong.

The Christian's Triple Life – W. E. Geil, Melbourne Town Hall, 6th May 1902

Southern Cross, 9th May 1902, 540–542.

Every Christian lives three lives. A great many people think that a Christian lives only two lives – the one here and the one hereafter – but this is a mistake. Every Christian leads three lives, and these are lives of prayer.

First there is the social or outside life of prayer – the life for Jesus Christ lived in the view of those with whom you work and reside. This is the life described in the Bible text, "Let your light shine before men that they may see your good works, and glorify your Father which is in Heaven." We should have sufficient good works exposed to view and sufficiently well-lighted as not to require our friends to use spectacles or a microscope to see that we are Christians.

I once heard it said that an old backwoods preacher in the State of New York used to preach sermons four hours long. Well, I saw him one day. It seemed that he was a Baptist, and used to preach right along from eleven o'clock to three, so that the Methodist could not get use of the building, as it was the only one in that locality. Well one day I met him, and asked him if it was true he preached four-hour discourses. "No," he said in his honest backwoods style. "That is a lie. I never preach longer than two hours and a half." Now I want you all to preach long sermons. Not measured by the watch, but by the yard stick and the mile. Preach sermons just as long as the distance through which you move. If you live four miles from this building, for instance, when you start out, clap a Bible under your arm and bring it along – you will have preached a sermon four miles long. That is just a sample of what I mean when I say we are to expose our good works to view – not to please our self-esteem, but that God shall be glorified by the good deeds we do.

The second life of the Christian is the life of prayer in the home. We ought to live for God where they live who love us most. West, the great painter was sitting one day with his colors mixed, and his canvas on the easel ready to start painting. He was unable to begin, however, because he had not the right kind of brushes; but just while he was sitting there the household cat came rubbing up against his leg, purring as she passed along. Like a flash the thought struck him. "Why, here's the very brush I want," and stooping down he cut off the cat's tail and began to paint with it. He took advantage of the thing next to him. I tell you that there are opportunities for us Christians to turn our hands to good deeds right in the home. I have sometimes come across people who are very anxious to go out to the mission-field, and I have said to them, "You try your religion on the people at home, and, if it works all right there, then you might take some of it along to the heathen afar off."

I think the saddest sentence I ever heard in my life came from the lips of a young woman who was sitting in the front seat of one of my meetings. After the address I threw the meeting open for remarks, and this young woman stood up and said most solemnly, "I have just come from looking into my father's grave. But there is something harder than that." I immediately came to the conclusion that she meant it would be harder to look into the grave of her mother. But she went on to say, "The hardest thing of all is that I never heard my father pray." Oh, my friends, have you a prayerless, godless father? You be saved yourself, and lead the life of prayer in the home, and I venture to say that God will so work through you so that your father will pray. You fathers that are here, do you pray in your homes? If you have not done so, begin at once. Get down on your knees and ask God to forgive your sins and to pardon your neglect in the matter of family prayer in the past.

The third life of prayer is the secret prayer life, when you get alone with God; and let me tell you this; your prayer will kill your sins, or your sins will kill your prayer. Jesus did not teach His disciples how to make sermons, but he taught them how to pray. Another thing, folks always show the sort of company they keep. It doesn't take long for an observing person

Appendix 2

to tell what sort of company you associate with during the day and evening, and if you are much with Jesus Christ in prayer, folks will soon begin to point at you and say, "There goes a man who has been with Jesus and has learned of him." It is in this life of secret prayer, too, that you get power for service – I call it the place of thunder. It is there that God appears to you, and pours His Spirit into your life. When you go in alone to your room, no one sees you, and no one hears you but your heavenly Father. Let your heavenly Father speak to you in this place of secret prayer, and He will give you such power that you will be able to go out and bring your friends to Christ.

When I was in the old cathedral at Antwerp, I sat looking for three hours at Rubens' great masterpiece – a wonderful painting, for which £200,000 sterling has been offered and refused. While I was sitting there an artist came along, fixed up his easel, got his canvas ready, his paint-box open, and his brushes prepared. Then he took up a little magnifying glass which hung around his neck by a string, and carefully examined a tiny fraction of the great masterpiece, and repeated that little fraction on his own canvas. So, he went on, looking at the big picture with his glass, and copying it, bit by bit. But the thing that struck me most was the conduct of the multitude that streamed past while he painted on unheeding. Not one in ten of them gave more than a passing glance at Rubens' picture, but all of them gazed at the artist who was copying it – some even remaining for an hour to watch him work.

And as I noted this, I thought how like our human life this is. The only idea some people will have of Rubens' painting will be the representation of it by this artist, and this artist, so far as these people are concerned, is responsible for the true representation of the great master. And in the same way a great many people will get their idea of Christ from the manner in which we represent Him in our lives.

Ah, friends, we walk in the range of human vision. The multitude streams past us day by day. It is for you and me to give a very true representation of our Lord and Master. We must look much at the man on Mount Calvary. We must study the picture minutely, bit by bit, fraction by fraction, and then with the help of the Holy Ghost we shall be able to fashion our life, and live it after that wonderful example.

And you will have power for service. Some folks will say it is personal magnetism, born in you, that enables you to grip and hold your friends; but if you lead these three lives of prayer, the Holy Spirit will give you power to reach out and grip your friends for God.

When I was in London I went to the old City Road Chapel, where John Wesley used to preach. The old sexton's wife, who shows strangers round, took me into the church, and showed me the pulpit from which he used to preach. Then I went out alone into the churchyard, and stood by the grave where John Wesley was buried. Well, I am not a place worshipper, but when I stood beside that grave I took off my hat and bowed my head and prayed. It never struck me there was anything else to do at the grave of that man of prayer but to pray. Oh, the life of prayer is the life of power, and its force will be projected beyond the century in which you and I live.

Finally, I want to tell you an anecdote which I hope you will never forget. It was a great mass meeting at which I had been speaking. The meeting in the auditorium was closed. The great crowd with which the building had been packed were moving off. The folding doors which shut off a smaller room from the lecture hall were half open, to allow persons to go in for inquiry. By and by this smaller room was filled with inquirers – amongst them being an infidel newspaper publisher. I went in, and the first person I met was a dear little girl about eleven years of age. Her eyes had the sparkle of perfect health, and her face was bright and cheerful. I shook her hand and said, "Are you a Christian?" "Yes, sir," she sweetly replied – she had been converted at a friend's house but a little while before. I said, "Is your father a Christian?" "I have no father, sir," she said in her sweet, sympathetic voice. "Is your mother a Christian?" I asked. And then, more sweetly and sympathetically, yet as if her heart were breaking for a mother's love, she said, "I have no mother, sir." "Will you pray?" I asked. "Yes, sir." Then I said, "Friends, it is time to pray;" and we knelt down, infidel and all. Then the most wonderful prayer that I ever heard fell from the lips of that orphan child as she knelt there, with her hands together, and her dear little face all aglow, as if reflecting the glory of the face of Christ. "Father, help me to do as I am told, for Jesus' sake," was the prayer she spoke. I tell you, the infidel used his big white handkerchief to catch the tears that were streaming down his face. There was weeping all over the room as that fatherless, motherless, child prayed over again the prayer of Jesus in Gethsemane, in her own childish words.

If you ask me what to pray I will tell you – "Father, help me to do as I am told." God has told us here [holding up his Bible] what to do. He wants us to be freed from sin to be saved today. Oh, men and women, pray that prayer, ask your Heavenly Father to help you to do what He has told you, and keeps telling you to do. You need not fear but that He will guide you aright. First pray, "Father, help me to do as I am told," then go and live the three lives of the Christian, and you will become noble, unselfish, Christ-like men and women!

Three Fires – R. A. Torrey, Exhibition Building, 9th May 1902

Southern Cross, 16th May 1902, 586–587.

The first fire – based on Matthew 3:11 – "He shall baptize you with the Holy Ghost and with fire." This came to me in a peculiar way; I had just moved from one house into another in Chicago. Sitting, tired, at the close of a hard day, I picked up a leaflet, and found myself after a long reverie shaking all over. My eye rested on the headline of the leaflet:– "Wanted, a Baptism with Fire." Said I, "That's just what I want." One verse quoted kept ringing through my heart:– "He shall baptize you with the Holy Ghost and with fire." Next day I could hear this verse sounding out through all my work. Saturday night came – a night on which I always attended a prayer meeting in the vestry of my church. I said to the janitor before the meeting commenced: "It is written, He shall baptize you with the Holy Ghost and with fire." The janitor smiled a meaning sort of smile, and I thought, "He knows more about this than the parson." A stranger from London was to preach for me the following Sunday morning, and I in the evening. I asked the Lord for a text for evening, and could get nothing but this verse: "He shall baptize you with the Holy Ghost and with Fire." This didn't seem to me like an evening text – I had been accustomed to address believers in the morning, and the unconverted at night. Then two more texts came to me, both with fire in them. I preached, and in the after-meeting powers unseen came upon the congregation, and we had a great outpouring of the Spirit. I have since met people all over the world who were in my church that night, and recalled the memory of it to me. Not long ago a lady in China spoke to me of it. I am going to take the same subject and lines tonight.

He shall baptize you with the Holy Ghost and with fire. The first fire, then, is the fire of the Holy Ghost. Jesus Christ baptized His disciples with the Holy Spirit and with fire. We all know what it is to baptize with water, by sprinkling, pouring or immersion. But this is a baptism with fire. What does this fire mean? What is fire said in the Bible to do? What happened to the disciples at Pentecost? We read that they were all with one accord in one place, waiting to be endued with power from on high. Suddenly there came a sound as of a rushing mighty wind, and there descended on each a cloven tongue like as of fire, and they were all filled with the Holy Ghost. The tongue symbolized the baptism of fire. The symbol may have departed, but the reality remains. The promise is to you and to your children.

When I first preached this sermon, I said to God the night before: "How can I preach what I have not got?" I went on my knees before Him and waited. I got such a revelation of myself as I never had before of my meanness, selfishness and self-seeking. Christian men and women, don't we need that now? It is not a pleasant revelation, but it is a salutary one.

Fire refines and purifies. Water washes the outside; fire cleanses internally. Throw a piece of gold in the fire, and all the alloy, the dross in it will be consumed. The dirt on the outside of our lives we can get rid of by outward reformation; but the alloy, the sin, down deep in our hearts – how shall we get it off? The baptism of the Holy Ghost will refine a man in five minutes. It is a slow process getting rid of our sins in any other way, but a baptism of fire does it at once.

Fire consumes. We need burning out of our love of money, our love of the world, our desire for men's applause, our looking at newspapers for reports of our sayings and doings, our fear of man, our selfish ambition, our desire to be in the forefront, our stubborn obstinacy. And this baptism of fire will do it for us tonight. I knew a young woman who professed to be a Christian, though many doubted it; in fact, she sometimes doubted it herself. She was stubborn, proud, loud, obstinate – everything a Christian ought not to be. She was a member of our church Bible Institute, of which her uncle was president. Every Bible Institute member is required to go out among the poor, and help them to Christ. One day this girl had been out and was tired. She walked along the Lake Shore drive, and noted the beautiful homes along its course. "Ah!" she said to herself, "this is what I like; I have had enough of dirty old stairways and squalor." She went home fighting against the Holy Spirit. At the tea table, all in a moment the Holy Ghost and fire fell upon her. In an instant she ran across the room, threw her arms around a girlfriend who was staying with her and exclaimed: "I'm a volunteer for South Africa." The fire of the Lord had burnt up everything evil in her heart and life. So transformed was she henceforth in her views, purposes, ambitions, nay, in her very face, that her best and closest friends

Appendix 2

could hardly believe she was the same girl. Isn't that what you need? You have an unconverted husband perhaps; seek for this baptism of fire so to cleanse and transform you that he may be won, by the change, to accept your Master as his.

Fire illuminates. All light comes from fire. Daylight is the effect of the combustion caused by the sun. A baptism of fire – the fire of the Holy Spirit – will do more to deliver a man from heresy than a theological education. Let a man be baptized with this fire, and all 'higher criticism,' theosophy, agnosticism, skepticism at once go away. The baptism of fire makes the Bible a new book, with a glory gilding every page. Before a man gets this baptism, he would rather read the last new novel, aye, or even an old almanac, than the Bible. But when he gets the baptism, he will grudge every moment given to any other study. The young girl I spoke of just now – 'Jack!' we used to call her, and that will tell you what sort of a girl she was – came to me after the great change had been undergone, and said: "Do you know what has happened to me?" The best thing about it is that the Bible, which to me used to be the dullest of books, is now the sweetest. God shows me something new every day in the Bible. The whole Bible Institute was stirred by the marvelous change in this girl. And my friends, what you all need, and what we preachers all need, is the baptism of fire!

Fire warms. You stand over a glowing furnace with a bar of iron. It is cold and dark. But plunge it in the fire, and note the rapid change. It was cold and hard, but now it is malleable, red hot, at a white heat! How cold we preachers are! But let God take and plunge us in the fire of the Holy Ghost, and we glow with love for Him, and love for perishing souls. Yes, our great need today is the baptism of fire. We preachers come out with solid arguments and beautiful illustrations. We convince the intellect, but we don't melt the will. We need to be preachers on fire! Wesley, Whitefield, Brainerd, Moody were on fire; and when we get on fire all Australia will be melted. We need a choir on fire. This choir sings beautifully, and you applaud it heartily. But when our choir gets the baptism of fire, you will not applaud, but will burst into tears.

We need Church members on fire! The strangers visiting our churches would not be frozen to death. Why doesn't the working man go to church? Why? Because he doesn't like a refrigerator! If the working man found the rich man all aglow with love to God and man he'd come to church fast enough!

Appendix 2

Fire begets energy. Men of science tell us that, given heat, we can generate energy. What generates power in the engine. The fire in the fire-box. A man shows me an engine capable of doing any amount of driving, and yet there is nothing moving. Why? He takes me below and shows me the fire-box empty. It wants fire, and without that fire all its elaborate and splendid mechanism is powerless and valueless. I go into some of your churches. What splendid frescoes! What elaborately carved seats! What an effective choir! What a capable minister, with the diction of an Addison and the elocution of a Burke. What perfect organization! What a large and well-arranged Y.P.S.C.E.! Look around, and with all this grandeur, there is not a wheel in the whole instrument moving for the glory and kingdom of God! There is no fire there! What we need is the fire of the Holy Ghost. When the Church gets on its face before God, and cries out for the baptism of the Holy Spirit, the fire will come, and a great work will be done.

Fire spreads. In 1872, and old woman, known as Mother O'Leary, was one day milking a cow in Chicago, with a lamp on the ground beside her. The cow kicked the lamp over, the grass ignited, the flames spread, and in forty-eight hours only two buildings were left standing in Chicago. Yes, fire spreads; but no fire spreads like the fire of the Holy Ghost. If we get a great baptism of fire on this Mission, it will sweep right through Australia, India and Africa. Jesus Christ baptizes with the Holy Ghost and with fire. These ministers around me can baptize with water, by sprinkling, affusion, or immersion, according to the applicants' desire and their respective practice; but only the Holy Spirit can baptize with fire. John baptized with water, so do my brethren here, and so do I; but He shall baptize you with the Holy Ghost and with fire, and He is here waiting to do it.

The Second Fire. I base this portion of my address on 1 Corinthians 3:13 and 15. "Every man's work shall be made manifest; for the day shall declare it, because it shall be revealed by fire, and the fire shall try every man's work, of what sort it is. If any man's work abide which he hath built thereupon, he shall receive a reward. If any man's work shall be burned, he shall suffer loss; but he himself shall be saved, yet so as by fire." The fire of God is going to try the work of every confessing Christian. I come with a message to you that your work will be tried by fire. This church work, so-called, of fairs, festivities, and tomfooleries, degrading the Church to the level of a museum or a vaudeville, will it stand God's test, think you? No, it will go up like smoke. Good sermons, perhaps sermons that convert some, but preached for men's applause, will they stand God's test? No, they will go up like smoke. Solos, sung in the sweetest and best voice and style, but sung only for applause, will they stand God's test, as work for Him? No, they will go up in smoke. I had two leading lady singers in my church choir, one of whom came to me, after I had preached this sermon there, and said, "I never sang a solo purely for God's glory; I want this baptism of fire." They both got it, and became missionaries. I lost them, of course, from the choir, and I wish I could lose the whole of this great choir here tonight in the same way. All of you here in this hall who are working for Christ, will your work stand? Has it an unmixed motive.

The Third Fire. What this is may be found from 2 Thessalonians 1:7-9: "The Lord Jesus shall be revealed from heaven with His mighty angels, in flaming fire, rendering vengeance on them that know not God, and that obey not the Gospel of our Lord Jesus Christ; who shall be punished with everlasting destruction from the presence of the Lord, and from the glory of His power." This is the fire of eternal doom. Everyone here must know the fire from God, either the glowing baptism of the Holy Ghost, or the fire consuming imperfect, mixed-motived works, or the fire of everlasting doom. Many here have experienced the first, as all may, if they will; some will experience the second; and some, it is to be feared, the third.

I hear someone say, "Is this fire of doom a literal fire?" For the sake of argument, I will let you take it as figurative; but remember, God's figures stand for facts, and His figures do not overstate His facts. Then, what agonies must be those which can be compared to 'smoke of torment ascending up for ever and ever'?

No exegesis can read out from the Bible the doctrine of endless punishment for those rejecting the Gospel of Christ. Did you ever burn yourself seriously? If so, you know the pain it brings. Now, think of such suffering enduring year after year, century after century, eon after eon, even to the ages of ages! Shallow thinkers say, "Oh! This can't be true." But don't you see men suffering here year after year, with no hope, if they reject the Gospel? If the day comes when repentance is impossible, what remains but an endless hell? You say you can't believe it. Your belief or not belief [sic] does not alter God's fact. The Christian Scientist says there is no such thing as pain; but you stick a pin in him, and see what he will say then. Remember, you don't get rid of a fact by denying it.

For whom is this doom? For them "that know not God." A man tells me he is an agnostic – he "does not know." Well, "know not" is English; agnostic, Greek; and ignoramus, Latin. Let him take his choice.

Appendix 2

Jesus Christ will render vengeance. You say, "this is not just." But it is a fact, and it is just. You ought to know God. You have resisted every attempt to bring you to know Him. You have put yourself under infidel influence; you have listened to blasphemous, obscene teaching. You ought to know God. It is your first and most solemn duty and obligation. If you are an honest and pure-mouthed agnostic, you can get rid of your trouble. I will show you how, if you will come to me after this meeting. I have never yet met an honest agnostic or Unitarian that I could not convince.

"And that obey not the Gospel." Many a man theoretically believes the whole Bible, from Genesis to Revelation, but does not "obey the Gospel." He will have the same fate as the agnostic.

All here must take choice between these three fires I have spoken of. Which do you choose?

Appendix 3
Spots

On the 'Eight Hours Day' public holiday on which it had been feared that the overflowing daytime services of other days would not eventuate, large crowds nevertheless gathered and a 'Bible-marking program' was demonstrated by W. E. Geil who claimed it as "one of the most remarkable schemes" ever invented.[1] Attendees were given small pieces of gummed paper, black, red, and yellow in color, referred to as 'spots.' The Mission committee's thorough preparations clearly ensured sufficient supply.

Seven pieces of gummed paper of each color were placed in three thousand envelopes to be moistened and attached to pages containing key verses of interest. The black pieces were doubled over and placed in the Bible to protrude from the edges of pages referencing sin, where the relevant verses were marked at the start and end with two perpendicular black lines. The black spot verses so marked were Job 25:4, Psalm 14:2-3, Proverbs 20:9, Ecclesiastes 7:20, Isaiah 64:6, John 3:18, and 1 John 3:8-10. Geil would indicate that the reading of the fifth black spot verse would allow "ample opportunity to speak with an unsaved person about his own righteousness."[2]

The red spots were intended to similarly protrude and represent Christian salvation, referencing the blood of Christ's atonement. The red spot verses were Isaiah 1:18, Matthew 1:21, Matthew 11:28, John 3:14-15, John 14:6, Acts 4:10, and Revelation 22:17. Each was marked at the start and end with a bracket to differentiate the verses from those associated with the black spots.

---

1. Geil, *Ocean and Isle*, 305.
2. Geil, *Ocean and Isle*, 307.

Appendix 3

The yellow spots represented prayer, or a divine solution to the problems of spiritual opposition. Again, doubled and placed to protrude, the verses were marked with pairs of parallel diagonal lines at the start and end. Verses denoted by yellow spots were Psalm 34:15-17, Psalm 1:15, Psalm 114:18-19, Matthew 21:22, John 14:13-14, Romans 8:34, and Romans 10:13.

Using a practical "blend of truth" from collective selections of individual verses to support an orthodox view of Christian salvation, Geil advocated their use with the unconverted friends of attendees, in leading to his challenge to have them kneel in prayer and to "call upon the name of the Lord for salvation."[3]

---

3. Geil, *Ocean and Isle*, 309.

Appendix 4
Letter to Hannah MacNeil

The following letter was occasioned by the passing of John MacNeil who had led his Prayer Band since 1889 seeking the spiritual awakening in Melbourne which eventually came in 1902. The band continued its weekly prayer after MacNeil's death. The letter was published in Hannah MacNeil's biography of her husband (*John MacNeil*, p. 394-395).

Letter from the "Band" – Melbourne, September 4th, 1896.

Dear Mrs. MacNeil,

"He maketh the storm a calm, so that the waves thereof are still." – Ps. cvii. 29. We, the members of the Melbourne "Band," of which Mr. MacNeil was for so many years the devoted and honored secretary, cannot let this season of your deep affliction pass away without a united message of profound sympathy.

What your husband was to the whole people of Australia, as a man evidently sent from God, who seemed to stand ever in full view of Eternity, and who was for ever engaged in seeking their salvation, we know, at least, in part.

What he was to the Church at large as the stern enemy of error, laxity, or compromise; as the eloquent advocate of whole-hearted self-surrender, and as a pattern of patient endurance and joy in service, we know in fuller measure.

What he was to ourselves as a loving companion, leader, champion, and torch of heavenly flame, we are only just beginning to realize.

Appendix 4

But what he was to you and to your children we can only faintly imagine.

We are well aware that we cannot estimate the greatness of your loss or the depth of your sorrow, and we therefore only ask your permission to stand almost in silence side by side with your beloved Lord, who, while He is stooping down to wipe away your tears is also lifting up His hands to crown His servant's head with a wreath of undying glory. In that holy, solemn, compassionate presence, we wish to assure you that we desire nothing more earnestly than to drink more deeply, as Mr. MacNeil used to drink, from the Fountain of Zion's waters; to follow the Master more fully, as he used to follow, with cheerful, unfaltering step; to breathe, as he used to breathe, only, always, and altogether for his King; to die, as he died, in the very thick of battle; and to shine, as he shall shine, like the stars for ever and ever.

We wish, moreover, to express our confident belief that his name will never be forgotten in our Australasian Churches, and that his words will be re-echoed by his spiritual children as long as we are a nation.

And now reminding you, dear Mrs. MacNeil, that you stand in a relationship to God which was impossible before – even to God as "the Father of the fatherless and the God of the widow"; that the most exquisite balm for your grief will be found in seeking to enter more and more into your husband's joy, and in the perpetuation of his prayer for the "Great Revival"; in looking, as he used to look, for the glorious appearing of our Lord Jesus Christ, and in realizing that the separation is only for a "little while."

We are, yours in the blessed hope,

ALFRED BIRD,
W. Y. BLACKWELL,
SAMUEL CHAPMAN,
WILLIAM H. GEORGE,
EDWARD HARRIS,
J. EAST HARRISON,
MATTHEW G. HART,
W. H. HOSKEN,
EDWAARD ISAAC,
S. C. KENT,
SAMUEL KNIGHT,

Appendix 4

CHARLES LANCASTER,
H. B. MACARTNEY,
D. S. MACCOLL,
D. O'DONNELL,
THOMAS PORTER,
JOSEPH ROSS,
GEORGE SOLTAU,
GEORGE SPROULE,
E. S. SUMNER,
JOHN WATSFORD,
ALLAN W. WEBB,
W. WILLIAMS.

Appendix 5
Mission Districts
(Published in The Age 12th April 1902, 14.)

214 Churches, 700 on local committees, 2,500 in choirs, 16,800 home preparation meetings with 117,000 attending, 50 centers, 50 missioners. Mr. W. Edgar Geil of Philadelphia, Dr. R. A. Torrey of Chicago, with Mr. Charles Alexander, American singer, will conduct noon meetings for businessmen daily, except Saturdays, from 1 to 1:45 p.m. and also afternoon Bible talks in Melbourne Town Hall. Meetings held in Suburbs daily, except Saturdays (with italics indicating required replacements).[4]

District	Site	Missioner
Ascot Vale	Tent – cnr. Union Rd. and the Parade	Rev. J. East Harrison
Albert Park	Tent – cnr. Kerford Rd. & Richardson St.	Rev. J. Watsford
Armadale	Hall	Rev. M. G. Hart
Collingwood	Town Hall	Rev. Dr. T. Porter (N.S.W.)
Clifton Hill	Tent – Mayor's Park	Rev. T. B. Tress
Brunswick	Tent – Sydney Rd.	Rev. D. C. Davidson M.A. (America)

4. Missions at Sandringham, Malvern East and North Melbourne followed. A Sandringham tent was erected with Rev. E. H. Shanks as speaker, being funded by residents (*Southern Cross*, 31st May 1902, 3). Plans were also made for a mission in Mentone from 15th June with C. F. Crosby of the Box Hill mission. Well-attended missions were also held in Williamstown (*Williamstown Chronicle*, 14th June 1902, 3) and Newport (*Williamstown Chronicle*, 24th May 1902, 3).

Appendix 5

Brighton	Drill Room	Revs. T. Tait M.A., B.D. & F. E. Harry
Box Hill	Federal Hall	Mr. C. F. Crosby
Carlton	Tent – cnr. Grattan and Cardigan Streets	Rev. F. Duesbury (N.S.W.)
Carlton North	Tent – cnr. Amess & Richardson Streets	Rev. E. H. Shanks B.Sc. (America)
Coburg	Shire Hall	Rev. C. H. Barnes & Mr. J. C. Langley
Camberwell	Shire Hall, Camberwell	Rev. T. S. B. Woodful
Elsternwick	Elsternwick Hall	Rev. S. Lenton (S.A.)
Essendon	Tent – Elstern Paddock, Buckley St.	Rev. W. T. C. Storrs M.A.
Fairfield Park	Fairfield Hall	Mr. James Robertson
Fitzroy	Exhibition Hall, Brunswick St.	Rev. J. Nall *and* E. Harris, *A. R. Edgar*
Fitzroy North	Tent – St. George's Rd.	Rev. W. A. Phillips
Footscray & Yarraville	Federal Hall	Mr. W. Edward Geil, D.C.L. (America)
Hawthorn	Town Hall	Rev. R. A. Torrey, D.D. (America)
Hawthorn West	Tent – St. James's Park Reserve	Rev. A. J. Clarke (S.A.)
Kew	Tent – High St.	Revs. R. Bavin (N.S.W.) & A.R. Edgar
Kensington, Flemington	Tent – cnr. Parson and Rankin Streets	Rev. D. O'Donnell
Moonee Ponds	Town Hall	Rev. J. H. Mullens (N.S.W.)
Malvern	Town Hall	Rev. W. L. Morton (S.A.)
Malvern East	Cairns' Memorial Church	Rev. S. Byron, W. Fitchett, E. Sugden
Melbourne South	Tent – cnr. Moray St. and Moray Pl.	Rev. W. Y. Blackwell M.A.
Melbourne West	Tent – cnr. Spencer and Hawke Streets	Mr. Robert Robertson
Melbourne North	Tent – cnr. Dryburgh and Erskine Streets	Rev. F. Harry, G. Mackay, & J. Virgo.
Northcote	Town Hall	Rev. D. M. Berry M.A.
Port Melbourne	Town Hall	Mr. W. H. Scurr

Appendix 5

Prahran & Windsor	Tent – High St.	Rev. G H. Bullen (N.S.W.)
Preston	Shire Hall	Rev. E. Isaac
Prince of Wales Park	Cnr. High St. and Darebin Rd.	Rev. J. Blakey (Tas.)
Richmond Central	Tent – 49-61 Coppin Rd.	Rev. S. C. Kent
Richmond South	Tent – cnr. Balmain and Chestnut Streets	Rev. J. Carson
Richmond North	Tent – cnr. Church and Ross Streets	Rev. A. Stewart M.A.
St. Kilda & Balaclava	Town Hall	Rev. Dr. Bevan
South Yarra & Hawksburn	Tent – Commercial Rd.	Revs. A. W. Webb (died) & G. H. Cole
Canterbury	Goulding's Hall	Revs. A. E. Albiston M.A. & D. Ross
Toorak	Jackson Street Hall	Rev. Robert McGowan
Williamstown & Newport	Tent – cnr. Fergusson and Cecil Streets	Commissioner McKie
Surrey Hills	Surrey Hall	Rev. G. McKay

Appendix 6
Summary of Suburban Mission Reports

Paraphrased from *Southern Cross*, 11th April 1902, 407–409, with notes from 18th April 1902, 427, and 25th April 1902, 459.

Albert Park (tent mission held at the corner of Kerford Road and Richardson Street). Rev. J. Watsford – a long-serving Methodist and primary figure in the Sydney Mission of 1901. Up to 800 attended the services, with 115 inquiries on the Tuesday evening at which only 400 attended overall.

Armadale (mission held at the Armadale Hall). Rev. M. G. Hart – former Tasmanian and Melbourne-based minister and current minister of a Presbyterian church located in the regional goldfields township of Ballarat. 500 attended the Sunday afternoon services and up to 350 at the evening sessions.

Ascot Vale (tent mission held at the corner of Union Road and Ascot Vale Parade). Rev. J. East Harrison – a Melbourne Baptist minister, formerly Congregational, with a recognized evangelistic gift. Up to 800 attended the sessions.

Box Hill (mission held at Federal Hall). Mr. C. F. Crosby – a merchant with a special interest in evangelism secured because of his "special aptitude" for the Mission at hand. Up to 320 attended the sessions, but with most being Christians.

Brighton (mission held at the Brighton Town Hall). Rev. T. Tait– a local Presbyterian minister and lecturer in theology at Ormond College affiliated

Appendix 6

with the University of Melbourne. Rev. F. E. Harry (also at Melbourne North) – a regional minister based in the regional township of Ballarat and president of the Christian Endeavor Union.

Brunswick (tent mission held at Sydney Road). Rev. D. C. Davidson – an American traveling evangelist with experience in missions on England and Scotland as well as other Australian states. Attendances were reported as exceeding 2,000 each night.

Camberwell (mission held at Federal Hall). Rev. T. S. B. Woodful – a recent returnee from a northern Victorian pastorate.

Canterbury (mission held at Golding's Hall). Rev. A. E. Albiston – a local, young Methodist minister. Rev. D. Ross – a local Presbyterian minister, having previously served interstate. Up to 300 in attendance at services with claims of a well-organized event.

Carlton (tent mission held at the corner of Grattan and Cardigan Streets). Rev. F. Duesbury – a prominent interstate Methodist evangelist. Attendance on the first Sunday afternoon was 300 with up to 800 attending in the evenings.

Carlton North (tent mission held at the corner of Amess and Richardson Streets). Mr. E. H. Shanks (Carlton North) – an American preacher and temporary lay-leader of a local Baptist church. Up to 700 attended the evening sessions, but it was believed that there were a higher proportion of those not usually attending churches who were present by the Tuesday evening.

Clifton Hill (tent mission held at Mayor's Park). Rev. T. B. Tress – a prominent local Anglican minister and evangelist. Up to 750 attended each service.

Coburg (mission held at the Coburg Public Hall). Rev. C. H. Barnes – former secretary of the Evangelical Church Association. Attendances approached 500 at services.

Appendix 6

Collingwood (mission held at the Collingwood Town Hall). Rev. Dr. T. Porter – a previous minister of Victorian churches, well known locally, but visiting from Sydney. 1,500 were reportedly present on the first Sunday evening with hundreds turned away.

Elsternwick (mission held at the Elsternwick Public Hall). Rev. S. Lenton – an interstate Congregational Church minister and supporter of the Y.M.C.A. Up to 600 in attendance in the evening sessions, with an average of 400. More than 20 percent were reported to be non-churchgoers from the earliest days of the mission and numbers were turned away from the venue on the middle Sunday of the event.

Essendon (tent mission held on Buckley Street). Rev. W. C. T. Storrs – a local Anglican vicar originating from England. Up to 800 attended the evening sessions with a large proportion being non-churchgoers. Numbers exceeded 1,000 at each of the Sunday services. Meetings for prayer were held between 7:30 and 8:30 am and 130 attended a prayer meeting on the middle Sunday. Bible readings were then held at 3pm on the Tuesday and Thursday and children's services were conducted at 4pm on the Wednesday and Friday.

Fairfield Park (mission held at the Fairfield Park Public Hall). Mr. James Robertson – experienced missioner serving with the Evangelization Society of Australasia. Up to 400 attended the services.

Fitzroy (mission held at Exhibition Hall). Rev. John Nall – another regional minister from Ballarat previously committed to evangelistic work with the Wesleyan Church. Rev. A. R. Edgar (and at Kew) – a local minister described as "the most beloved man in the Methodist Church of Victoria." Rev. Henry Howard – local Methodist minister and later associate minister of the Fifth Avenue Presbyterian Church in New York. Services held up to 600 people, but with 1,200 on the first Sunday evening and 1,500 on the following at which Henry Howard preached and "ten or twelve" came to faith.

Fitzroy North (tent mission held at the corner of Rae and Scotchmer Streets). Rev. W. A. Phillips – a local Anglican vicar with extensive prior experience in Sydney. A maximum of 350 people were accommodated in

APPENDIX 6

the tent in each service but with a further 200 present outside at the Sunday evening service.

Footscray (mission held at Federal Hall). Mr. W. E. Geil – a keynote mission speaker and international explorer from Pennsylvania. Attendances averaged 1,300 per evening session with more than one hundred acceptance cards signed in each. Overflow seating was available at the Royal Hall with more than 700 extra people present.

Hawthorn (mission held at the Hawthorn Town Hall). Rev. R. A. Torrey – the keynote speaker of the mission overall, from Chicago. Attendances were at the maximum of 1,200 for each session, with overflow seating provided at a nearby church hall. A large number of non-churchgoers were present. A feature of the services was said to be the singing led by Charles Alexander.

Hawthorn West (tent mission held at St. James' Park Reserve). Rev. A. J. Clark – an evangelist with experience in three states, having been commended by Charles Spurgeon as "the most promising evangelist" he had ever sent. Up to 650 attended the sessions with the tent's side flaps lifted to accommodate the overflow, although most attendees were believed to be Christians.

Kensington (tent mission held at the corner of Parson Street and Rankin Road). Rev. David O'Donnell – an experienced evangelist involved in the Sydney Mission in the previous year. Up to 1,300 attended the evening sessions.

Kew (tent mission held at High Street adjoining the Salvation Army barracks). Rev. Rainsford Bavin – a prominent interstate Methodist and father of a later state premier. Rev. A. R. Edgar (and at Fitzroy) – a local minister described as "the most beloved man in the Methodist Church of Victoria." Rev. John Barnaby – a local Presbyterian minister. Attendances averaged in excess of 700 but with a large proportion of churchgoers. A Friday evening prayer meeting was held from 10:30 to 12:30 and a large open-air service was then held at 8 pm at the Post Office on the middle Saturday of the event. A men's meeting of 400 gathered on the Sunday afternoon and 1,200 were present at the Sunday evening service and hardly any standing room remained available outside the tent. The *Southern Cross* recorded a nearby publican claiming his business had been "spoilt" by the event.

Malvern (mission held at the Malvern Town Hall). Rev. W. Lockhart Morton – an interstate minister with local experience in the Presbyterian Church. In excess of 500 were present at services.

Melbourne East (mission held at the Cairns Memorial Church, East Melbourne – site also listed as Malvern East). Rev. S. Byron – a regional Victorian Presbyterian minister and singer. Rev. E. H. Sugden – a Methodist minister associated with Queen's College affiliated with the University of Melbourne. Rev. Dr. W. H. Fitchett – Methodist President and editor of the "Southern Cross" newspaper.

Melbourne North (tent mission held at Dryburgh Street, North Melbourne). Rev. F. E. Harry (also at Brighton – a regional minister based in the regional township of Ballarat and president of the Christian Endeavor Union.

Melbourne South (tent mission held on Moray Street, South Melbourne). Rev. W. Y. Blackwell – a principal of a local training home for missionaries. Up to 700 attended evening services.

Melbourne West (tent mission held at the corner of Spencer and Hawke Streets). Mr. Robert Robertson – an interstate evangelist associated with the Evangelization Society of Australasia. 800 were present on the first Sunday afternoon and up to 650 in the evenings with 94 inquirers at the conclusion of the Tuesday evening session, inclusive of 66 children.

Moonee Ponds (mission held at the Moonee Ponds Town Hall). Rev. J. H. Mullens – an evangelist engaged in ministry with an interstate Anglican congregation. Up to 1,200 attended the evening sessions.

Northcote (mission held at the Northcote Town Hall). Rev. Digby M. Berry – an Anglican minister associated with the Evangelical Church Association. Average attendances at services were 150 with most being adult churchgoers.

APPENDIX 6

Port Melbourne (mission held at the Port Melbourne Town Hall). Mr. Will H. Scurr – a speaker associated with the Evangelization Society of Australasia and ministry to young people.

Prahran (tent mission held on High Street). Rev. D. H. Dillon (also listed as Rev. G H. Bullen) – a Sydney minister involved in its 1901 Mission. Afternoon attendance on the first Sunday was 2,000 with up to 1,800 attending the evening sessions, with 187 inquirers at the conclusion of the Tuesday evening session.

Preston (mission held at Shire Hall). Rev. E. Isaac – a local Baptist minister originally from England. Attendances of up to 500 at the evening services were exceeded on the first Sunday afternoon, when 1,000 children and 200 adults were present.

Richmond Central (tent mission held at Coppin Street). Rev. S. C. Kent – a local Anglican minister involved with the Sydney Mission and elected as deputy chair of the Melbourne Mission's Central Committee. After a small opening attendance of 150 on the first Sunday afternoon, 800 were present in the evening service and up to 500 in the following services.

Richmond North (tent mission held at the corner of Ross and Church Streets). Rev. J. Carson – an evangelist and local Baptist minister. Up to 700 were present at the evening services, where it was noted that "the percentage of unconverted among the audience [was] increasing."

Richmond South (tent mission held at the corner of Balmain and Chestnut Streets). Rev. A. Stewart – the minister of a large local Presbyterian church. Up to 750 attended services at which half were estimated to be people not usually attending churches.

St. Kilda (mission held at the St. Kilda Town Hall). Rev. Dr. L. D. Bevan – the minister of Melbourne's Congregational Church with prior experience in England. In excess of 1,000 attended the Sunday afternoon and evening services, with up to 500 present on weekday evenings.

South Yarra (tent mission held on Commercial Road). Rev. Allan W. Webb – the minister at the Baptist church of the major regional township of

Appendix 6

Geelong and convenor of the first Keswick conventions there. Services exceeded 1,000 but with 2,100 present on the first Sunday evening, including mostly Christians in attendance. Webb died on the Wednesday morning of the event.

Surrey Hills (mission held at Surrey Hall). Rev. G. Mackay – a Tasmanian Baptist minister and singer. Up to 250 were present at the evening services.

Thornbury (tent mission held at the corner of High Street and Darebin Road). Rev. J. Blaikie (also listed as J. Blakey) – an interstate Baptist minister, formerly associated with a local congregation. Up to 400, and an average of 250, attended the evening sessions including many young people. Progress was reported as follows: "Addresses earnest, attention held, conviction awakened, surrenders many, inquirers more, workers alert!"

Toorak (mission held afternoons at the Presbyterian Hall and evenings at the Jackson St. Hall). Rev. Robert McGowan – a minister from a regional Victorian Presbyterian church. Audiences exceeded 100 in services.

Williamstown (tent mission held at the corner of Ferguson and Cecil Streets). Commissioner Thomas McKie – head of the Salvation Army in Australia and a prominent evangelist. 2,200 attended the first Sunday afternoon, with up to 1,200 at the evening services, a large proportion of which were not church attendees. Extra services were held for children at Newport and Spotswood and "72 stood up for salvation."

Appendix 7

Program for Torrey and Alexander Valedictory Meetings

Farewell service for Torrey and Alexander held on Monday 6th October 1902 in the Melbourne Town Hall with an overflow service in the Independent Church (now St. Michael's Uniting Church, Melbourne). Programs were recorded in the *Southern Cross*, 10th October 1902, 1156.

TOWN HALL MEETING				INDEPENDENT CHURCH MEETING			
Chairman – REV. PEARCE CAREY				Chairman – A. R. EDGAR			
Choir - MR. ALEXANDER		Mins. 30	7.00 to 7.30	Choir - MR. MORGAN		Mins. 25	7.00 to 7.25
Prayer - REV. KENT		5	7.30 to 7.35	Prayer -		5	7.25 to 7.30
Report by Secretary - Mr. CHAS. CARTER		10	7.35 to 7.45	Choir - MR. ALEXANDER		20	7.30 to 7.50
				Report by Secretary - Mr. CHAS. CARTER		10	7.50 to 8.00
Music Selection		5	7.45 to 7.50				

Appendix 7

Address -			Music Selection	5	8.00 to 8.05	
REV. P. CAREY	10	7.50 to 8.00				
			Address -			
Choir -	5	8.00 to 8.05	Rev. A. R. EDGAR	15	8.05 to 8.20	
MR. ALEXANDER						
			Choir -	5	8.20 to 8.25	
Address -	25	8.05 to 8.30	MR. MORGAN			
DR. TORREY						
			Address -	15	8.25 to 8.40	
Collection -	10	8.30 to 8.40				
Organ Solo			Collection -			
Resolution of thanks	5	8.40 to 8.45	Choir – MR. MORGAN	10	8.40 to 8.50	
to Dr. and Mrs. Torrey and Mr. Alexander			Address DR. TORREY	25	8.50 to 9.15	
Address – Resolution	15	8.45 to 9.00				
Rev. C. H. NASH Mr. G. P. BARBER			Choir - MR. MORGAN	5	9.15 to 9.20	
Choir -	10	9.00 to 9.10	Resolution -			
MR. ALEXANDER			REV. THOS. TAIT HON. JAS. BALFOUR	5	9.20 to 9.25	
Benediction			Benediction			

Bibliography

Books and Articles

Abrams, Minnie. "How the Recent Revival Was Brought About in India." *Latter Rain Evangel* 1 (1909) 6–13.

Alexander, Helen Cadbury and J. Kennedy Maclean. *Charles M. Alexander, A Romance of Song and Soul-Winning*. London: Marshall Brothers, 1920.

Anderson, Allan. *An Introduction to Pentecostalism*. Cambridge: Cambridge University Press, 2004.

———. "Pandita Ramabai, the Mukti Revival and Global Pentecostalism." *Transformation* 23 (2006) 37–48.

Babbage, S. Barton and Ian Siggins. *Light Beneath the Cross: The Story of Billy Graham's Crusade in Australia*. The World's Work: Melbourne, 1960.

Bartleman, Frank. *Azusa Street: The Roots of Modern-Day Pentecost*. South Plainfield: Bridge, 1980.

Bennett, David. *The Altar Call: Its Origins and Present Usage*. Lanham: University Press of America, 2000.

Berry, Digby. "The Great Australian Revival No. 2." In *Ocean and Isle*, edited by W. E. Geil, 282–304. Pater: Melbourne, 1902.

Bickford, James. *Christian Work in Australasia*. London: Wesleyan Conference, 1878.

Blainey, Geoffrey. *The Heyday of the Churches in Victoria*. Melbourne: Uniting Church Historical Society, 1985.

Blamires, W. L. and John B. Smith. *The Early Story of the Wesleyan Methodist Church in Victoria*. Melbourne: Wesleyan Book Depot, 1886.

Bruner, Frederick Dale. *A Theology of the Holy Spirit*. Grand Rapids: Eerdmans, 1970.

Carey, S. Pearce. "The Conspiracy of Circumstances." In *Ocean and Isle*, edited by W. E. Geil, 243–57. Pater: Melbourne, 1902.

Chant, Barry. *The Spirit of Pentecost: The Origins and Development of the Pentecostal Movement in Australia, 1870-1939*. Lexington: Emeth, 2011.

———. *This is Revival*. Tabor: Sydney, 2013.

———. "Wesleyan Revivalism and the Rise of Australian Pentecostalism." In *Reviving Australia: Essays on the History and Experience of Revival and Revivalism in Australian Christianity*, edited by Mark Hutchinson, Edmund Campion and Stuart Piggin, 97–122. Center for the Study of Australian Christianity: Sydney, 1994.

Coghlan, T.A. *A Statistical Account of the Seven Colonies of Australasia, 1901-1902*. Sydney: Commonwealth, 1902

BIBLIOGRAPHY

Davis, George. *Torrey and Alexander: The Story of a World-Wide Revival.* New York: Fleming H. Revell, 1905.

———. *Twice Around the World with Alexander, Prince of Gospel Singers.* New York: The Christian Herald, 1907.

———. "Views of the Famous American Missioner About the Great Religious Awakening in England and Wales." *Sunday Strand* 12 (1905) n.p.

Dorsett, Lyle W. "D. L. Moody: More than an Evangelist." In *Mr. Moody and the Evangelical Tradition*, edited by Timothy George, 31–8. London: Continuum, 2004.

Drake, E. T. *Victorian Year Book, 1905.* Melbourne: Government Statist of Victoria, 1906.

Dyer, Helen S. *Pandita Ramabai: The Story of Her Life.* New York: Fleming H. Revell, 1900.

———. *Revival in India: Years of the Right Hand of the Most High.* London: Morgan and Scott, 1907.

Evans, Eifion. *The Welsh Revival of 1904.* Bridgend: Evangelical, 1987.

Evans, Robert. *Evangelism and Revivals in Australia: 1880-1914.* Self-published: Sydney, 2005.

Faupel, William. *The Everlasting Gospel.* Dorset: Deo, 2009.

Finn, Edmund ("Garryowen"). *The Chronicles of Early Melbourne: 1835-1852.* Melbourne: Fergusson and Mitchell, 1888.

Geil, William Edgar. *Ocean and Isle.* Pater: Melbourne, 1902.

———. *A Yankee in Pygmy Land.* London: Hodder and Stoughton, 1905.

Gloege, Timothy E. W. *Guaranteed Pure: The Moody Bible Institute, Business, and the Making of Modern Evangelicalism.* Chapel Hill: University of North Carolina Press, 2015.

Graham, Billy. *Just as I Am: The Autobiography.* Sydney: Harper Collins, 1997.

———. "The Second Coming." Audio recorded February 1959 in Melbourne, Australia. Charlotte: Billy Graham Evangelistic Association, 1959.

Grant, James and Geoffrey Serle. *The Melbourne Scene: 1803-1956.* Sydney: Hale and Ironmonger, 1983.

Harkness, Robert. *Reuben Archer Torrey: The Man ... His Message.* Chicago: The Bible Institute Colportage Association, 1929.

Hayter, Henry Heylyn. *Victorian Year Book, 1887-1888.* Melbourne: Government Statist of Victoria, 1888.

———. *Victorian Year Book, 1892.* Melbourne: Government Statist of Victoria, 1893.

———. *Victorian Year Book, 1889-1890.* Melbourne: Government Statist of Victoria, 1891.

Jackson, H. R. *Churches and People in Australia and New Zealand 1860-1930.* North Sydney: Allen and Unwin, 1987.

Jupp, James. "Salvationists." In *Encyclopedia of Religion in Australia*, edited by James Jupp, 554–60. Melbourne: Cambridge University Press, 2009.

Lloyd-Jones, D. Martyn. *Joy Unspeakable: The Baptism with the Holy Spirit.* Eastbourne: Kingsway, 1984.

Maclean, J. Kennedy. *Torrey and Alexander: The Story of their Lives.* London: S. W. Partridge, 1905.

Marsden, George M. *Fundamentalism and American Culture: The Shaping of Twentieth-Century Evangelicalism, 1870-1925.* Oxford: Oxford University Press, 1980.

Martin, Roger. *R. A. Torrey: Apostle of Certainty.* Murfreesboro: Sword of the Lord, 1976.

McCrindle, Mark. *The Changing Faith Landscape of Australia.* Norwest: McCrindle Research, 2022.

Bibliography

McLean, W. *Victorian Year Book 1902*. Melbourne: Government Statist of Victoria, 1903.

———. *Victorian Year Book 1903*. Melbourne: Government Statist of Victoria, 1904.

———. *Victorian Year Book 1904*. Melbourne: Government Statist of Victoria, 1905.

Nienkirchen, Charles W. *A. B. Simpson and the Pentecostal Movement*. Peabody: Hendrickson, 1992.

No Author. *Alexander's Revival Songs*. Melbourne: T. Shaw Fitchett, 1902.

No Author. *Annual Pastoral Address and Minutes of the First Victoria and Tasmania Annual Conference of the Methodist Church of Australasia 1902-1905*.

Orr, J. Edwin. *Evangelical Awakenings in the South Seas*. Minneapolis: Bethany, 1976.

Packer, J. A. "The Great Australian Revival No. 1." In *Ocean and Isle*, edited by W. E. Geil, 258–81. Pater: Melbourne, 1902.

Paproth, Darrell. "Revivalism in Melbourne from Federation to World War I: The Torrey-Alexander-Chapman Campaigns." In *Reviving Australia: Essays on the History and Experience of Revival and Revivalism in Australian Christianity*, edited by Mark Hutchinson, Edmund Campion and Stuart Piggin, 143–69. Sydney: Center for the Study of Australian Christianity, 1994.

Penn-Lewis, Jessie. *Awakening in Wales*. Dorset: The Overcomer Literature Trust, n.d.

Piggin, Stuart. "Towards a Theoretical Understanding of Revival: Recent Developments in the Historiography of Revival." In *Reviving Australia: Essays on the History and Experience of Revival and Revivalism in Australian Christianity*, edited by Mark Hutchinson, Edmund Campion and Stuart Piggin, 13–33. Center for the Study of Australian Christianity: Sydney, 1994.

Piggin, Stuart and Robert D. Linder. *Attending to the National Soul: Evangelical Christians in Australian History, 1914-2014*. Monash University: Melbourne, 2020.

———. *The Fountain of Public Prosperity: Evangelical Christians in Australian History, 1740-1914*. Monash University: Melbourne, 2018.

Pollock, John. *Moody: A Biography*. Grand Rapids: Baker, 1997.

Ravenhill, Leonard. *Why Revival Tarries*. Minneapolis: Bethany, 1959.

Robeck Jr., Cecil. *Azusa Street Mission and Revival: The Birth of the Global Pentecostal Movement*. Nashville: Thomas Nelson, 2006.

Satyavrata, Ivan. "Contextual Perspectives on Pentecostalism as a Global Culture: A South Asian View." In *The Globalization of Pentecostalism: A Religion Made to Travel*, edited by Murray Dempster, Byron D. Klaus and Douglas Peterson, 203–221. Oxford: Regnum, 1999.

Schmidgall, Paul. *European Pentecostalism: Its Origins, Development, and Future*. Cleveland: CPT, 2013.

Scotland, Nigel. "Towards a Biblical Understanding and Assessment of Revival." *Evangelical Quarterly* 85 (2013) 121–34.

Selby, Isaac. *The Memorial History of Melbourne*. Melbourne: The Old Pioneers Memorial Fund, 1924.

Shaw, Mark. *Global Awakening: How 20th-Century Revivals Triggered a Christian Revolution*. Downers Grove: Intervarsity, 2010.

Stead, W. T. *The Welsh Revival: Narrative of Facts*. Boston: Pilgrim, 1905.

Stibbe, Mark. "No Limits, No Boundaries." In *Breakout: One Church's Amazing Story of Growth Through Mission-Shaped Communities*, edited by Mark Stibbe and Andrew Williams, 219–44. Milton Keynes: Authentic Media, 2008.

Synan, Vinson. "Missionaries of the One-Way Ticket." In *Azusa Street and Beyond: Missional Commentary on the Global Pentecostal/Charismatic Movement*, edited by Grant McClung, 41–52. Alachua: Bridge-Logos, 2012.
Tidball, Derek. "'A Work so Rich in Promise': The 1901 Simultaneous Mission and the Failure of Co-operative Evangelicalism." *Vox Evangelica* 14 (1984) 85–103.
Torrey, Clara. Diary, 23rd June 1902. Archives of the Billy Graham Center, Wheaton College, Illinois. Ephemera of Reuben Archer Torrey – Collection 107.
Torrey, R. A. *The Baptism with the Holy Spirit*. New York: Fleming Revell, 1895.
———. *The Power of Prayer and the Prayer of Power*. New York: Fleming H Revell, 1924.
Treloar, Geoffrey. "The First Global Revivalist? Reuben Archer Torrey and the 1902 Evangelistic Campaign in Australia." *Church History* 90 (2021) 873–99.
Virgo, John J. *Fifty Years of Fishing for Men*. London: Pilgrim, 1939.
Warren, William. "The Genesis of the Australian Revival." *The Missionary Review of the World* 16 (1903) 200–3.
Watsford, John. *Glorious Gospel Triumphs as Seen in My Life and Work in Fiji and Australasia*. London: Charles H. Kelly, 1901.
Watson, David L. and Paul D. Watson. *Contagious Disciple Making: Leading Others on a Journey of Discovery*. Nashville: Thomas Nelson, 2014.
Whittaker, Colin. *Great Revivals*. London: Marshall Pickering, 1990.

Newspapers and Magazines

Age
Argus
Australian Town and Country Journal
Ballarat Star
Bendigo Advertiser
Bendigo Independent
Catholic Press
Ecclesiastical Observer
Herald
Illawarra Mercury
Illustrated Australian News
Institute Tie
Leader
Leaves of Healing
Missionary Review of the World
Port Melbourne Standard
Punch
Southern Cross
Spectator
Sunday Times (Perth)
Sydney Morning Herald
Watchman
Weekly Times
Williamstown Chronicle

www.ingramcontent.com/pod-product-compliance
Lightning Source LLC
Chambersburg PA
CBHW051058160426
43193CB00010B/1236